Death
Defying Acts

Woody Allen
"Central Park West"

David Mamet
"An Interview"

Elaine May
"Hotline"

3 One-Act Comedies

A SAMUEL FRENCH ACTING EDITION

SAMUEL FRENCH
FOUNDED 1830

SAMUELFRENCH.COM

IMPORTANT BILLING AND CREDIT REQUIREMENTS

All producers of DEATH DEFYING ACTS *must* give credit to the Authors of the Plays in all programs distributed in connection with performances of the Play and in all instances in which the title of the Play appears for purposes of advertising, publicizing or otherwise exploiting the Play and/or a production. The name of the Authors *must* also appear on a separate line, on which no other name appears, immediately following the title, and *must* appear in size of type not less than fifty percent the size of the title type, substantially as follows:

(Name of Producer)
Presents
"DEATH DEFYING ACTS"

Woody Allen	David Mamet	Elaine May
"Central Park West"	"An Interview"	"Hotline"

3 One-Act Comedies

VARIETY ARTS THEATRE

Under the Direction of Ben Sprecher and William P. Miller

JULIAN SCHLOSSBERG and JEAN DOUMANIAN

PRESENT

LINDA LAVIN   DEBRA MONK   PAUL GUILFOYLE

DEATH DEFYING ACTS

WOODY ALLEN
"CENTRAL PARK WEST"

DAVID MAMET
"AN INTERVIEW"

ELAINE MAY
"HOTLINE"

3 NEW ONE-ACT COMEDIES

AASIF MANDVI   PAUL O'BRIEN   TARI T. SIGNOR

AND

GERRY BECKER

SCENIC DESIGN	COSTUMES	LIGHTING
ROBIN WAGNER	JANE GREENWOOD	PETER KACZOROWSKI
SOUND	PRODUCTION SUPERVISOR	CASTING
JAN NEBOZENKO	STEVEN ZWEIGBAUM	STUART HOWARD/ AMY SCHECTER
PRESS REPRESENTATIVE	GENERAL MANAGEMENT	ASSOCIATE PRODUCERS
BONEAU/ BRYAN-BROWN	RICHARD FRANKEL PROD./ MARC ROUTH	LETTY ARONSON MEYER ACKERMAN

DIRECTED BY

MICHAEL BLAKEMORE

CAST

(in order of appearance)

AN INTERVIEW

The Attorney ....PAUL GUILFOYLE
The Attendant ....GERRY BECKER

HOTLINE

Ken ....GERRY BECKER
Dr. Russell ....PAUL GUILFOYLE
Marty.. PAUL O'BRIEN
Dorothy ....LINDA LAVIN
Delivery Boy ....AASIF MANDVI

FIFTEEN MINUTE INTERMISSION.

CENTRAL PARK WEST

Phyllis ....DEBRA MONK
Carol ....LINDA LAVIN
Howard ....GERRY BECKER
Sam ....PAUL GUILFOYLE
Juliet ....TARI T. SIGNOR

STANDBYS
Standbys and understudies never substitute for listed players unless a
specific announcement for the appearance is made at the time of the performance.

For Dorothy, Carol, Phyllis—Lauren Klein; for the Attorney, Dr. Russell,
Sam—Chuck Stransky, Paul O'Brien; for the Attendant, Ken,
Howard—DanDesmond; for Juliet—Jennifer London; for Marty,
Delivery Boy—Dan Desmond, Chuck Stransky.

CONTENTS

AN INTERVIEW

by

David Mamet

AN INTERVIEW

(AT RISE: A LAWYER and an ATTENDANT sitting in Hell.)

ATTORNEY. Well. Alright. Shall we begin? *(Pause.)* Mmm? No? *(Pause.)* What is the issue? *(Pause.)* Alright. Is, um, well, fine. I'll begin. Fine. Did, I, I *put* it to you: did I not serve others well.

ATTENDANT. ... did...

ATTORNEY. Yes. Did I not act *honorably,* and...

ATTENDANT. ... did.

ATTORNEY. ... I'm not finished.

ATTENDANT. Forgive me.

ATTORNEY. ... honorably, in the discharge of *all* duties *remotely* contained under the Laws Governing Agency.

(Pause.)

ATTENDANT. I'm afraid you'll have to expl...

ATTORNEY. ... did I not?

ATTENDANT. ... Did...

ATTORNEY. ... in all matters affecting the Welfare of Another.

ATTENDANT. ... waal...

ATTORNEY. ... excuse me, *which he had put in my charge.*

ATTENDANT. ... which he had put in your charge.

ATTORNEY. Yes. Professional, or personal, or...

(Pause.)

ATTENDANT. For example?
ATTORNEY. Well, well, they're not lacking.
ATTENDANT. Alright.

(Pause.)

ATTORNEY. An example?
ATTENDANT. Yes.
ATTORNEY. Alright. An Example--of acting in others' best interest. For example: Fine: A Loan.
ATTENDANT. A Loan. Of... ?
ATTORNEY. ... of... of... of. A loan, of: a *lawnmower.*
ATTENDANT. Alright.
ATTORNEY. ... When...
ATTENDANT. ... did someone actually loan you a lawnmower?
ATTORNEY. ... did they...
ATTENDANT. ... yes.
ATTORNEY. I'm sure they did. I..
ATTENDANT. ... can you... I don't mean to *antagonize* you...
ATTORNEY. Go on...
ATTENDANT. ... but...
ATTORNEY. Did they Loan Me a Lawnmower.
ATTENDANT. Yes.
ATTORNEY. ... in contradistinction to, to...
ATTENDANT. ... to your...
ATTORNEY. ... my, yes, my merely *hypothesizing* such a loan, as...

ATTENDANT. ... that's right.

ATTORNEY. ... an example of...

ATTENDANT. ... that's right.

ATTORNEY. ... a picturesque example of...

ATTENDANT. ... the "sort" of transaction...

ATTORNEY. ... yes. Yes. Yes. Did someone Loan Me a Lawnmower. *(Pause.)* I am prepared to... I don't know. I don't... wait. I don't know. I am prepared to *stipulate*, mmm? Whichever you...

ATTENDANT. ... I don't...

ATTORNEY ... that I *did,* or *didn't*...

ATTENDANT. ... didn't... ?

ATTORNEY. Borrow...

ATTENDANT. ... mmm?

ATTORNEY. You see?

ATTENDANT. No.

ATTORNEY. I am prepared to... whichever you,... *choose.* Do you see? Choose. Choose. Mm? I don't remember. *(Pause.)* I don't remember, *if, in, fact,*

ATTENDANT. ... but...

ATTORNEY. Yes. Alrig... yes. Fine. Alright. I *was* lent a lawnmower.

ATTENDANT. You were.

ATTORNEY. Yes.

ATTENDANT. You were?

ATTORNEY. Yes. How about that. In my youth. It seems. I mowed "lawns" with it. Yes I did. I borrowed a neighbor's "lawnmower" on one occasion.

ATTENDANT. Why?

ATTORNEY. Well, it would have been mine was broken...

ATTENDANT. ...mmm...

ATTORNEY. ... and I'm sure that I returned it, in Better Shape--no, I won't be grandiose--in a state *as good as* that in which I'd found it. And I'll Tell You Why! That man, my Father's Friend, the man next door, from whom I'd borrowed it--isn't it strange what we recur to? As I *took* it, I told him. "I'll treat it like it was my own." And he said, "No. Treat it as if it's mine." Now: can I think that that comment didn't *influence* me? Over the Years...? And I cite the Very Fact that it was buried, to support my thesis.

(Pause.)

ATTENDANT. What was buried?

(Pause.)

ATTORNEY. I'm sorry?
ATTENDANT. What was buried? *(Pause.)* The Lawnmower?

(Pause.)

ATTORNEY. You're joking.
ATTENDANT. What?
ATTORNEY. You're joking.
ATTENDANT. No.

(Pause.)

ATTORNEY. ... was the lawnmower buried?

(Pause.)

ATTENDANT. Yes.

(Pause.)

ATTORNEY. ... you're joking. *(Pause.)* Who would bury a lawnmower? *(Pause.)* Do you see my point?

ATTENDANT. Who'd Bury a Lawnmower?

ATTORNEY. Yes.

ATTENDANT. I don't know. *(Pause.)* Who *would* bury a lawnmower?

ATTORNEY. *(Pause.)* No one I know.

ATTENDANT. But you said that it was buried.

ATTORNEY. ... mm...

ATTENDANT. ... you said...

ATTORNEY. ... I said the *comment* was buried.

ATTENDANT. ... the comment.

ATTORNEY. Yes.

ATTENDANT. What comment?

ATTORNEY. The "thing" the man said.

ATTENDANT. It was buried.

ATTORNEY. Yes.

ATTENDANT. What do you mean?

ATTORNEY. ... it... I *forgot* about it.

ATTENDANT. Yes. I'm sorry. I've forgotten it, too. Could you...

ATTORNEY. He Said "treat it As If It Were Mine".

ATTENDANT. Yes. Yes. Yes. I'm... he lent you the lawnmower, and *you* said...

ATTORNEY. I said I'd treat it as if it were my own.

ATTENDANT. Yes.

ATTORNEY. And *he* said: "No. No. Treat it as if it were *mine.*" *(Pause.)* "Mine", meaning "his".

ATTENDANT. It was his, though. *(Pause.)* It was his... wasn't it?

ATTORNEY. Yes.

ATTENDANT. Alright. Yes. Alright. So. I see. He meant "Treat it With the Respect Which It Deserves."

ATTORNEY. Yes.

ATTENDANT. He said that.

ATTORNEY. Yes.

ATTENDANT. .. You forgot it.

ATTORNEY. No. Not *then.* MMM? I forgot it *subsequently.* I *didn't* forget it. I *suppressed* it. Mmm? As in *hydraulics* where the very act of the *suppression* causes it to rise, with greater *force.* You see? In my subconscious.

ATTENDANT. You, you , you found it profound that he asked you to treat his lawnmower with respect?

(Pause.)

ATTORNEY. I had mouthed a *platitude*...

ATTENDANT. ... mmm?

ATTORNEY. And he suggested, through *wit,* that that which, to my infant mind, was *meaningful,* might be discarded in favor of a more mature philosophy.

ATTENDANT. He was suggesting that you treated your own gardening tools less-than-well? *(Pause.)* Was he?

ATTORNEY. Well, he may have been.

ATTENDANT. How did that make you feel?

ATTORNEY. I don't remember.

ATTENDANT. Can it have made you "proud"?

ATTORNEY. No, I can't think so, though...

ATTENDANT. ... or "Happy".

ATTORNEY. I... no, no, no, no, I see your point.

ATTENDANT. Perhaps it enraged you?

ATTORNEY. Yes. Yes. I see where you're...

ATTENDANT. ... and that is why you suppress it.

ATTORNEY. ...mmm.

ATTENDANT. ... and your whole business life has been the effort to repay that man for your humiliation.

ATTORNEY. Heh heh.

(Pause.)

ATTENDANT. Maybe you did bury the lawnmower.

ATTORNEY. "Maybe" I did, yes. But I didn't.

ATTENDANT. Why did you, alright, then, why did you say "maybe I did"?

ATTORNEY. I was agreeing with you.

ATTENDANT. Yes, but why...

ATTORNEY. ... I was agreeing with you... it's a "debating" device, if you will. To agree to the *lesser*... Abraham *Lincoln* did it. *Cicero* did it. To grant that which can not be successfully disputed, thereby gaining credibility, for those few objections one *may* fruitfully make.

ATTENDANT. Why could it not be successfully disputed?

ATTORNEY. Why, why could what not?

ATTENDANT. That you had buried the...

ATTORNEY. ... is that, now, is that what we were...

ATTENDANT. ... yes.

ATTORNEY. Refresh me.

ATTENDANT. I said "Maybe you buried the lawnmower", and you said as how you'd grant me that, as it could not be successfully disputed.

(Pause.)

ATTORNEY. Well. It could not.
ATTENDANT. Why?
ATTORNEY. ... because, because... How...
ATTENDANT. You could have said, "No, I didn't."
ATTORNEY. How would I prove it?
ATTENDANT. Are you suggesting that that which cannot be documented must be abjured?

(Pause.)

ATTORNEY. Can't we drop it?
ATTENDANT. If you wish.
ATTORNEY. Thank you.
ATTENDANT. ... through you're the one that brought it up.
ATTORNEY. I'm aware of that.
ATTENDANT. ...n'I must suppose you raised it for a reason.
ATTORNEY. Yes, ah, well, no, there's no such thing as "Randomness", that the thing...?
ATTENDANT. How would I know? *(Pause.)* Hm. You were saying?
ATTORNEY. I'm sorry. Is there someone else I could talk to?
ATTENDANT. No.

ATTORNEY. I don't *mind*, do you see? Being treated, in the hackneyed phrase, "just like everybody else", in fact, had it been given me to choose I would have *requested* such treatment... that I *not* be granted special favors. And I am, in fact, *glad* that this is being conducted on a "level playing field". Mmm? Like the sons of the Rich, I would hate to feel that my *distinction* was owing to factors not of my control. Do you see, and, so, then, to suffer anxiety about whether my preferment was, in fact, deserved...

ATTENDANT. ... I'm listening.

ATTORNEY. I do not, as I said--nor is it given me, and, I must say, *nor do I feel that I require* preferment, preferential "treatment", or, or, or "grading on a Curve". Nor do I ask for such. Nor do I ask for such. But I must say that I feel that the, the, the, the *components* of the interchange, You and "I", in effect, that, it may be said "Are Not a Good Mix". ... where is the shame in that? And, so, I ask if I might, purely at random, do you see--I don't ask, and I *would* not ask, even if it were given to me, which it is not, and which is a situation I endorse, for the reasons--and think it specious of me, if you will, but I believe I've stated my position on them--I do not ask to, to "speak to your Superior", or any of that, "Hogwash". But I would like, at the risk of offending you--though why should I, for neither of us has done anything remotely construable as giving offense--I would like to be returned to the "pool", if you will, if such exists, and if I use the right term, to take my chances, being assigned randomly, as I assume it is done, and if it costs me a... *seniority* of any sort, so be it--to be assigned to another, well, if I may, to another interviewer. *(Pause.)* Might we... *(Pause)* Might we do that?

(Pause.)

ATTENDANT. No.

(Pause.)

ATTORNEY. Yes. I expected your response, and I endorse it. But: if I might state my reasons... mmm? No...? "I've Said Them"? Hm. Alright. Good. Fine. Well, fine. I've said it, and it "clears the Air". And one lesson of business, I feel, and it is in divergence from the most Accepted Belief, and, perhaps, for that *reason* has served me so well--it's founded not on *theory*, but on observation is: It Is Not Necessary To Be Liked. *(Pause.)* That may be heresy to you, I know it was to many in my field. I presume that it conjures images of disgraceful behavior; of *discourtesy*. Of *"rudeness"*. But I put it to you: may not an *antipathy* occur from organic and *legitimately* differentiating interests? Of *course* it can. In business...--what is business but the bringing together of dissimilar, or of *apparently* dissimilar mm...? What? Goals. Is it essential that two parties...

ATTENDANT. No, you've lost me.

ATTORNEY. What?

ATTENDANT. You've lost me.

ATTORNEY. I was saying... *(Pause.)* Where did you... Where did I lose you...?

ATTENDANT. At the beginning.

ATTORNEY. ... the beginning.

ATTENDANT. Yes.

ATTORNEY. Of what?

ATTENDANT. Of the whole thing.

(Pause.)

ATTORNEY. ... I...

ATTENDANT. Why did you bury the lawnmower?

ATTORNEY. *Fine.* I'd like to... "recast" my remarks. May I do that?

ATTENDANT. I don't know what you mean.

ATTORNEY. I'd like to... to "recast", to "re-*state*" my, in answer to your question, I would like to...

ATTENDANT. ... what question...?

ATTORNEY. You asked me... you asked me... you... you aren't going to help me.

ATTENDANT. *(Pause.)* No.

ATTORNEY. You asked me, you suggested that I *may* have buried the lawnmower.

ATTENDANT. Yes.

ATTORNEY. And I agreed.

ATTENDANT. Mm.

ATTORNEY. No, alright, and Why Would I have Agreed, had I *not,* in fact, done that Heinous Thing.

ATTENDANT. Yes.

ATTORNEY. That's your Question.

ATTENDANT. That's one of them.

ATTORNEY. Heh heh. Then we're going to be here awhile. Is that it? *(Pause.)* Is that it? Is that the thing? We're going to be here a wee while, and can go "nowhere" until we dispose of this point. Is that the thing? I've brought it up, and, so, it, what, we have to, is that the thing?

ATTENDANT. Yes.

ATTORNEY. Thanks for your candor. That's it. Let me ask you: what *weight*, then , does the assertion have?

ATTENDANT. That you buried the lawnmower?

ATTORNEY. Yes.

ATTENDANT. What weight?

ATTORNEY. If it were to be proved.

ATTENDANT. How could one prove it?

ATTORNEY. Mmm. Quite. If I *admitted* it...?

ATTENDANT. Is it true?

ATTORNEY. Let's just, for a second, say, that, under certain circumstances, I might *say* that it's true.

ATTENDANT. Why?

ATTORNEY. To "move this Thing Along". Eh?

ATTENDANT. You'd swear to what was false?

ATTORNEY. I'd...

ATTENDANT. ... you'd...

ATTORNEY. I'd "fib", alright? I'd "fib". You're going to tell me that you don't know what a "fib" is? It's a "lie", alright...? It's a "White Lie"... a "white Lie is a Lie", yes. Alright. Yes, yes, yes, yes, and I'm suggesting that I'd do it. What a Bad Man. What a Bad Bad Man. No. Never seen his like. What a Tale for the Boys at the Club. What a sad reminiscence for the odd Commemorative Banquet. "I cannot discharge from my mind the instance, singular, in all my service, of a man, I can not couch it so's to Spare your Feelings... but... He Told a Fib" *(Pause.) HA? (Pause.) HA? (Pause.)*... Oh, the hell with it. I buried the Lawnmower.

ATTENDANT. Next Case.

ATTORNEY. Let me retrace my steps a moment. We live in a World of Norms. It may be unfortunate, but it is so. I feel we always have. That norm once supplied by the Church is gone... "If you act Otherwise than As God Wills it, you are Lost". That's gone. But let's examine it a moment, if we might.

... I shun the philosophic argument, and proceed to the social... That Person who ignored the dictates of the Church did so at immediate risk of social ostracism--leaving, as I say, the question of perpetual, et cetera--Now: that Norm's Vanished, but, but... Mass *Media,* do you see, *supplant* it. We are not *told* of Salvation, but *shown* it, and Not To Live Up To That Norm, brings not *guilt,* no. Not *Guilt,* but *Anxiety.* We strive, therefore, to live up to that Norm. Not to do so is to court Anguish. No, I don't think that's too strong a word... this *second,* where was I...?

ATTENDANT. ... I don't know.

ATTORNEY. ... two norms. Alright? Social Behavior. Standards. ... all founded, whether the *Church,* or the Lines of a New Car, on--though they may *contain* truth, on, on an *arbitrary,* for what is truth?

ATTENDANT. ... what is truth?

ATTORNEY. Yes.

ATTENDANT. What?

ATTORNEY. "What is truth"?

ATTENDANT. Yes.

ATTORNEY. What?

ATTENDANT. Who knows.

ATTORNEY. "Who knows what 'truth' is?"

ATTENDANT. Yes.

ATTORNEY. Who?

ATTENDANT. Who? I don't know. You brought it up.

ATTORNEY. Alright. Is there such a "thing" as Truth? *If* there is Such a Thing as Truth... you see, I say "If", if there is such a thing. If truth exists, then, in truth, I know the truest thing I know is this: I never buried a lawnmower. *(Pause.)* I may have done *other* things. I'm sure that I did. I did things I *regret,* I will go so far, make of it what you will, as to inform you I did things which I despise. Which of us hasn't? Does that excuse them? No. Exonerate me? No. Not at all. I did them, I own up to them, if you would like to know what they are, ask me, and I will enumerate them. Does the urge to excuse myself render me corrupt? I do not *wish* to excuse myself. I wish, being human, to "present" myself, "warts And All". *Both* the good and the bad, and to receive fair, if I may, impartial, what, "enlightened"--if that falls to my lot--consideration. Am I willing to be educated? Yes. Am I willing to fawn, no. *(Pause.)* No. I am not. Ask me why, I can't tell you, save that I'm a man. I confess it. I lived, I sinned, I am not perfect. The list of my sins, if compiled...

ATTENDANT. Why did you bury the lawnmower?
ATTORNEY. I did *not* bury it.
ATTENDANT. Who did?
ATTORNEY. Who did? *No* one.

(Pause.)

ATTENDANT. How do you know?
ATTORNEY. Because I was there.
ATTENDANT. You were there. When?

(Pause.)

ATTORNEY. Alright. *(Pause.)* Alright. Fine. Fine. I buried the lawnmower. How Bad is That? I buried it. I did it, I'm guilty, put it down to my account. I buried it. I did it. Fine. Fine. "Rot in Hell". It can't be worse than this. I buried the lawnmower. *(Pause.)* I stole. *(Pause.)* I... *(Pause.)* I... I subverted the Judiciary. I misused my client's funds. *(Pause.)* I suborned perjury. I screwed little Dot Callahan, and left town. I don't even know if she got Pregnant. That's not the lot, but that's the tone of the thing. Eh? May I go now. Whatever the thing is. Fine. May I go?

ATTENDANT. Yes.

(ATTENDANT scribbles on a pad. Hands it to the ATTORNEY.)

ATTORNEY. *(Reads.)*"Eternity in Hell, bathed in burning white phosphorous, while listening to a Symphonic Tone Poem." Because of the Things I Had Done. Such a bad man. Fine. Just, just for my edification. What *particularly,* mm? Cause it looks to me like a Kangaroo Court. Mm? To what do I owe this sentence? Pray, what are they?

ATTENDANT. Two things. Either in itself, excusable. Both, in conjunction, requiring the punishment in Hell: You passed the Bar, *(Pause.)* and you neglected to live forever.

(Pause.)

ATTORNEY. You know, prejudice is a terrible thing. It can take many forms. Sexual, Racial, or, it seems, professional. I would not have thought it, but here you are prepared to damn a man because of supposed attributes of a profession to which he belongs. That's wrong. That's just wrong. Are you saying there are no honest lawyers? *(Pause.)* "No comment?"

ATTENDANT. Name me one.

ATTORNEY. Well, I'll tell you what. Are you a sporting man? I'll name you one. I will name you an honest lawyer. Mm? And then you apologize to me. And you set me free.

What do you say to that?

    ATTENDANT. Go ahead.

    ATTORNEY. How much time do I have?

    ATTENDANT. We hope that you'll like it here.

END OF PLAY

COSTUME PLOT

ATTORNEY
  3 Piece charcoal gray suit with suspenders
  Striped shirt w/French cuffs
  Silver and gold "A" cufflinks
  Silver and gold faux Rolex
  Yellow and red tie
  White carnation
  Black socks w/ribbing
  Black leather wingtip shoes
  Polo athletic T-shirts (under all)

ATTENDANT
  Black two piece suit
  Fray rigged shirt
  Maroon vest
  Black leather belt
  Plain black socks
  Black toe-cap shoes
  Toupee

PROPERTY PLOT

KILL RUNNING LIGHTS

Table with Drawer
   Props Inside Desk Drawer:
         Ashtray
         Wet Rag
         Spare Lighter
         Spare Pack of Cigarettes
         1 Pad Paper: 8 1/2 x 11 for *HOTLINE*
         1 Pencil for *HOTLINE*
2 Chairs
"NO SMOKING" Siogn
1 Pad of Paper
1 Pen
1 Pack Cigarettes on Table
1 Gold Lighter on Table

AN INTERVIEW

Stage Left

Chair

Cigarettes w/lighter

No Smoking Sign

Pad & Pen

Stage Right

Chair

HOTLINE

by

Elaine May

HOTLINE
TRANSCRIPTION FROM TAPE

The tape that precedes *Hotline* (The transcript of which is included here.) is only used when *Death Defying Acts* is presented in its entirety. It is played in the dark during the set change and its purpose is to make clear to the audience that it is not part of the first play.   —*Elaine May*

(Phone rings.)

   1ST VOICE. Hotline

(Phone rings.)

   2ND VOICE. Hotline.

(Phone rings.)

   3RD VOICE. Hotline.
   WOMAN'S VOICE #1. I'd like to talk to a counselor.
   MALE COUNSELOR'S VOICE #1. Tell me what's upsetting you.
   WOMAN'S VOICE #1. I just... I just don't see the point of anything.

(Phone rings.)

   HISPANIC MALE VOICE. Hello... Is there someone there I can talk to?
   MALE COUNSELOR'S VOICE #2. Yes, yes, I'm a counselor.
   HISPANIC MALE VOICE. Well... I'm very upset.
   MALE COUNSELOR'S VOICE #2. That's okay. Tell me about it.

(Phone rings.)

WOMAN'S VOICE. *(ADELE COOMBS.)* Is Adam there?

COUNSELOR'S VOICE. *(ADAM.)* Hi, Mrs. Coombs. This is Adam.

WOMAN'S VOICE. *(ADELE COOMBS.)* Adam? Oh, I'm so glad I got your phone. I'm going to do it again, Adam.

COUNSELOR'S VOICE. *(ADAM.)* Well, let's talk about it, Adele.

(Phone rings.)

FEMALE COUNSELOR'S VOICE. Hotline

ENGLISHMAN'S VOICE. Yes, I'd like to talk to someone about oral sex.

FEMALE COUNSELOR'S VOICE. What?

ENGLISHMAN'S VOICE. Oral sex.

FEMALE COUNSELOR'S VOICE. We're not that kind of hot line.

ENGLISHMAN'S VOICE. I'm sorry. I'm afraid someone has played a very cruel joke on me.

(Phone rings.)

1ST VOICE. Hotline

(Phone Rings.)

2ND VOICE. Hotline

(Phone rings.)

END OF TAPE

HOTLINE

(The stage is divided in half. Stage right is concealed by a closed slider panel. Stage left angles off into the wings as if it is part of a larger space.)

(KEN GARDNER is at a table L staring, anxiously, at two phones that sit side by side. The sound of muted voices, ringing phones, and moving shadows offstage give the impression that there are others at similar tables, answering similar phones.)

1ST VOICE. You must feel terrible, Linda. Would you like to tell me what's wrong?...

2ND VOICE. Hot line. ... I see. Why don't you tell me what's wrong?...

3RD VOICE. Hot line. ... Yes, I am. ... Well, that's what I'm here for. Tell me about it...

(KEN glances toward the voices, then adjusts his two phones so that they are exactly even. A middle-aged man in a suit enters behind him. He is Dr. Russell, the supervising psychologist.)

DR. RUSSELL. How's it going, Ken?

KEN. *(Whirling around.)* Oh! Dr. Russell. You startled me.

DR. RUSSELL. *(Chuckling.)* Scared the hell out of you is

what you mean. Let's say what we mean, Ken. If we're going to help others get in touch with their feelings we have to be honest about our own.

KEN. Right. *(Suddenly.)* And I'll tell you something else that's crazy. My phones haven't rung. And I feel it's because they know it's me. I feel they've *decided* to ring for the others because they know they're better at this than I am. I mean, I *know* it's insane and phones are electrical instruments...

DR. RUSSELL. That's fine, Ken. Be aware of that feeling. Of course, it's not a feeling you'll want to share with a disturbed person. But there can be a lot of resentment when you're talking to someone bent on self-destruction. Recognize it. *(He claps KEN on the back.)* Then keep it to yourself.

KEN. *(Calling after him.)* Dr. Russell! Do you think... would it be possible for someone to sit with me for the first couple of calls? In case I run into something over my head...

DR. RUSSELL. We're all in over our heads here, Ken. Just remember your Schneidman, your training, your seminars, and then follow your instincts.

KEN. Just... just for the first call? You see... I've never actually dealt with another human being in trouble. I mean, the... simulated situations are close, but these are real people. I mean... someone may actually live or die because of what I say on the phone.

DR. RUSSELL. If you feel that way, Ken, this is not the job for you.

KEN. *(Quickly.)* Right. I mustn't be arrogant.

DR. RUSSELL. Remember that what these people want most is someone to talk to, they want help, otherwise they wouldn't be calling. I'm not going to tell you that a rebuff or harsh treatment couldn't push someone over the edge. But they're not going to get that from you, Ken, because you're a trained counselor and an intuitive, intelligent human being. But you're not God.

KEN. Right. Thank you, Dr. Russell.

(DR. RUSSELL claps him on the shoulder again and walks off. KEN sits staring down at his phones. A 2nd counselor, MARTY, steps out of the shadows and speaks to him.)

MARTY. He's a great guy, isn't he, Russell? Sometimes when I get into something really messy I can hear his voice guiding me.

KEN. Yes... Were you this nervous before the first call?

MARTY. Oh, sure. Listen, we all were. But half the trick is just answering "Hot Line". I don't know why but it opens them right up, makes them feel safe. I don't know why...

(One of the phones on KEN'S desk suddenly lights up and begins ringing. KEN jumps, then stares at it, then picks it up.)

KEN. *(Into phone.)* Hot line. ... That's right. ... That's what I'm here for. Tell me what's wrong.

(DR. RUSSELL walks on behind KEN and stands quietly listening.)

KEN. Where are you now Eddie? ... I see. Well, if you come in off the ledge I think we'll be able to hear each other better. ... Well, I'll tell you what, why don't you climb back in through the window and I'll keep talking, so you'll know I'm still on the line and you don't have to answer, okay?... What would you like me to say? ... Anything? Okay. Let's ... give it a try. *(Raising his voice, slightly.)* ... My name is Ken Gardner and I'm sitting in a room that's about 14 by 25, and I'm behind a table that's about 2 by 4 and I'm talking to you, and I'm going to keep on talking to you while you climb back through the window--very carefully--because I'd like to talk to you after you get inside and find out what's troubling you... and you don't have to rush, Eddie, you can go back through the window, very slowly and carefully, because I'm going to be here, Eddie, talking to you for as long as it takes, so just... *(His voice suddenly returns to normal.)* ... Hello, to you. ... Well, good. I feel much better now, too. *(He chuckles.)* ... No, that's alright, you rest. That's a good idea. It's exhausting to do what you just did. ... No, no, you call me back whenever you feel like it. I'll be here all night. And I'm proud of you, Eddie.

(He hangs up. MARTY and DR. RUSSELL burst into applause... then Dr. Russell makes an "O" with his thumb and forefinger and goes off.)

MARTY. You did great.
KEN. *(Awed.)* I saved a life.
MARTY. It's a great feeling, isn't it?
KEN. I've never felt anything like this before.
MARTY. There's nothing like it. I've worked in drug centers, I've worked with battered wives...
KEN. It's a *great* feeling!
MARTY. ... but these people are so vulnerable. It tears your heart out.

(The lights fade up on DOROTHY R, who sits, motionless, staring into a hand mirror as the right panel opens.)

KEN. Yes! That's it. The vulnerability. I loved that guy. I've never felt so close to anyone... in... in just that way. He was so lost. And I was all he had. I was *it.*

MARTY. Yes.

KEN. *They're* the ones who are nervous. So scared you'll smash their last little hope...

DOROTHY. *(Into the mirror.)* What the fuck are *you* looking at.

KEN. ... so timid and... grateful.

(The lights go out on KEN and MARTY and the left panel closes.)

(DOROTHY puts the mirror down, empties a bottle of pills into a glass bowl, pours a glass of water, then picks up the phone and dials 411. The lights come back up stage L as she dials and the left panel opens part way, revealing KEN on the phone, speaking with much more ease and a certain authority.)

KEN. ... what would you *like* to hear me say, Hal?...

DOROTHY. *(Into phone.)* I'd like the telephone number of The Suicide Center. ... In Manhattan. ... There's more than one suicide center? In Manhattan? ... Well, which one is actually called The Suicide Center?

KEN. ... I don't think you're a bad person, Hal.

DOROTHY. I don't understand. You mean there are five suicide centers in Manhattan and none of them is called The

Suicide Center? ... No, no, listen. I want the main suicide center.
It would be an emergency listing--like the Fire station. ... Right.

KEN. ... No, I don't think that's evil, Hal. Just human.

DOROTHY. ... Well, are all five of them listed the same
way? ... Then you're not checking right. Listen, operator, this
is a very special listing, you follow? This is for morte. Yo
morte. So you go now, and look for the number of The Suicide Center, not "A" Suicide Center because "The" is part of
the name. "El". El center por yo morte.

KEN. ... Well, maybe she was upset, too. You know, small
things can look awfully big when they all come at the same
time.

DOROTHY. ... No, that's not it, operator. ... You've checked
every emergency listing? ... So what you're telling me is that
in all of Manhattan the only place officially listed as The Suicide Center is a coffee house. ... Fine. Thank you. Can I speak
to someone who isn't Spanish.

KEN. ... I'll be here all night, Hal, so if you start feeling
bad again you just call me. My name is Ken, and I'll be here
for you. *(He chuckles.)* ... Okay, Hal, you, too.

*(KEN hands up and leans back, contentedly, as the lights fade
out and the stage left slider closes.)*

DOROTHY. *(Into phone.)* ... Yes, you can. I've been trying
to get the telephone number of The Suicide Center from one
of your operators who can barely speak English and who has
informed me that out of the dozens of suicide centers now
lining Manhattan the only one called The Suicide Center is a
coffee house. Now, I go through this shit almost every time I
call Information but I usually let it pass because I go through

so much shit every time I do anything that I hate to single out one special group. But this is an emergency. This is the kind of thing where if you don't get a number you can die. And I don't think you people should hire Information operators who will be handling life and death emergency cases unless they have some grasp of the language of your customers. ... Yes, you can. I want the telephone number of The Suicide Center. In Manhattan. ... Hello? ... Oh, sorry. I thought you were gone.

(There is a knock on the door.)

    VOICE. *(Calling.)* Burger shop!
    DOROTHY. Oh, shit. *(Calling.)* Just a minute. *(Into phone.)* ... It's an emergency listing. Like a Fire Station. ... No, it would be called The Suicide Center. Listen, who is this? Are you the same operator I just talked to pretending not to have an accent? ... Well, I don't believe this. You mean you don't have one listing for The Suicide Center? ... Where is that? ... No, that's the number I just got. That's the coffee house.
    VOICE. *(Calling.)* Burger shop!
    DOROTHY. *(Calling.)* Wait a minute, will you? I'm on the phone. *(Into phone.)* Well, who would know. Who do you suggest I call now that Information is stumped. ... Is that 911? ... The Police Emergency number--is that 911?
    VOICE. *(Calling.)* Should I come back with this?
    DOROTHY. *(Calling.)* Will you wait a fucking minute! *(Into phone.)* ... 911? ... The Police Emergency is 911?... Thank you, you moron.

(DOROTHY hangs up, dials 911. We hear the faint sound of a busy signal. There is another knock.)

DOROTHY. Shit! Hold on! Fuck. Just a second.

(She hangs up, dials "0", then, still carrying the phone, she goes to the door, unlocks it, and opens it. A Delivery Man stands there with a bag.)

DOROTHY. How much is it? *(Into phone.)* Operator, I wonder if you can help me. I just dialed 911 for Police Emergency and I got a busy signal. ... Yes, I know that means it's busy. I wondered if you could break in on the conversation for me. This is an emergency. *(She picks up her purse from a table as she speaks.)* But they're not all as *much* of an emergency. ... No, we can't know that. Thank you. Your simple wisdom has saved me from doing a very selfish thing. *(She hangs up and dials 911 again. There is the faint sound of ringing; to the Delivery Man.)* How much is that?
    DELIVERY MAN. Seven-fifty.
    DOROTHY. For a hamburger?
    DELIVERY MAN. And coffee. You got coffee, too.

(DOROTHY fishes in her purse, the phone still to her ear, takes out bills and change and counts them into his hand.)

DOROTHY. ... that's three... four... four-twenty... four-thirty-five... *(Into phone.)* Answer, you bastards! *(To DELIVERY MAN.)* How much did I give you so far?
    DELIVERY MAN. Four-thirty-five.
    DOROTHY. Four-thirty-five? And I owe you seven-fifty... so seven-fifty minus four-thirty-five is...
    DELIVERY MAN. Three-fifteen.
    DOROTHY. *(Counting it into his hand.)* ... and another

fifty... and five... *(Into phone.)* Oh, hi. Jesus, thank God you
fellows have an emergency number, otherwise the guy who
just killed my husband would have gotten away while I called
some ordinary precinct. ... No, he stayed here and waited for
you to answer. We're watching the Robin Byrd show. ... Yes,
it's an emergency. But I'm only going to talk for a minute
because I don't want you to trace this call, so don't try to stall
me or I'll hand up. ... I'm going to kill myself and I can't get
the number of The Suicide Center from Information. Do you
have it? *(She hands the DELIVERY MAN a coin.)* What's that
clicking noise? You're trying to trace the call aren't you? *(She
turns her purse over and shakes out more coins.)* ... I don't
want anyone from my precinct to talk to me, I want to talk to
someone from The Suicide Center. *(Gives the DELIVERY MAN
more change.)* Look, what's the number of the place you call
when you're going to commit suicide and they talk to you on
the phone and try to get you to change your mind? There was
a movie about it with Sidney Poitier about ten years ago and it
played on television last month. And there was an article about
it in the Post a couple of weeks ago. That's the one. And Poitier
played the worker. Right. ... Thank you. Just let me find
something to write this on. *(She grabs a kleenex and pencil
from an end table.)* Slowly, please. ... 6-0066. Thanks. And
I'm going to thank you in my note. *(Hangs up; to DELIVERY
MAN.)* How much more do I owe you?

DELIVERY MAN. A dollar eighty-eight.

DOROTHY. Listen, this is all I can find right now. But I've
got some money here somewhere, I hide it from myself--what
time do you close?

DELIVERY MAN. Eleven.

DOROTHY. Oh, good. Well, I'll find it before then... and

I'll bring the dollar eighty-eight plus a tip down to the Burger Shop. Okay?

DELIVERY MAN. That's alright. I'll wait.

DOROTHY. I have to look for it. Hey, come on, you know where I live. I'm not going to leave town to get out of paying for a hamburger.

DELIVERY MAN. Yeah, but you're calling the cops and you're calling the Suicide Center... I'm taking it for granted you're not serious, but I made less than two dollars in tips today. I don't want to get stuck for a dollar eighty-eight...

DOROTHY. I'll find you the fucking dollar eighty-eight. And you can shove the hamburger up your ass for a tip.

(DOROTHY goes off.)

DELIVERY MAN. Thank you. I appreciate it.

(The lights come up and the L panel opens on KEN, talking on the phone.)

KEN. ... Well, I care, Barbara. ... Yes, very much. ... You call whenever you feel like talking and ask for Ken. I'm here all night. *(He chuckles.)* Okay.

(KEN hangs up. MARTY comes over and sits on the edge of the desk.)

MARTY. You're really good at this.

KEN. It's because I'm not trying. I really feel what I say. *(He leans back.)* You know, I'm not like this in life. I mean, in everyday life.

MARTY. Well, who is? You can't do this twenty-four hours a day.

KEN. It's not that I don't have compassion for people. I do. But I don't... I don't know what to say to them in life. Sometimes I feel so sorry for someone I can't look at him. You know what I mean?

MARTY. Sure. Because there's nothing you can do for him.

KEN. Well, maybe. I don't know. I tend to judge myself... harshly.

MARTY. That's very arrogant.

KEN. *(Quickly.)* Yes. I know. That's what Russell says.

MARTY. He's a brilliant son-of-a-bitch, isn't he?

KEN. He's a good man. I told him I thought he was a great man, but he said it was transference.

MARTY. That's what's so great about him. He has no vanity. Are you a psychologist?

KEN. I have an M.S. I was going to stay in research because I tend to be too... intense about people. I tend to want to help them too much... to save them. Russell told me to examine those feelings very carefully. It's amazing how much counseling is like Catholicism. You never know whether you're being a good Samaritan or committing the sin of pride. *(The phone rings. He reaches for it.)* Excuse me. I have to save a life.

(Then panel closes and the lights go out on KEN... and come up to full on DOROTHY, who is now taking coins out of a coffee can and counting them into the DELIVERY MAN'S hand.)

DOROTHY. ... a dollar seventy-eight, a dollar seventy-nine... That's it.

DELIVERY MAN. You don't have nine cents more?

DOROTHY. Fuck off.

DELIVERY MAN. Okay. I hope I haven't inconvenienced you. *(He starts out; stops.)* You know I saw that movie--the one about the suicide center--on T.V.

DOROTHY. Yeah? It was good, wasn't it?

DELIVERY MAN. Excellent. I thought it was one of the best things Poitier's done.

(He goes out. DOROTHY turns the radio up, dances over to the mirror, puts on lipstick and combs her hair.)

DOROTHY. *(Singing with the radio.)* "... These little town blues..."...

(She puts the radio down, picks up the kleenex with the number on it and dials.)

DOROTHY. ... Hi, is this The Suicide Center? ... Is this The Suicide Center? ... The hot line to what? To The Suicide Center? ... Look just tell me if this is The Suicide Center. I'm not interested in the branch. ... Yes, but I didn't ask you that. I didn't care about that. I just wanted to know if this was The Suicide Center. ... Don't say it again. I don't want you to say "hot" or "line" during this phone call, alright? ... Listen, I just called to tell you that you're not listed. Did you know that? Some asshole Puerto Rican Information Operator told me that there were five suicide centers listed and none of them was you. I had to call the police to get your number. ... I didn't say she was an asshole because she was Puerto Rican. I said she was an asshole *and* she was Puerto Rican. Just like you're an

asshole and you're not Puerto Rican. See how that works?...
Listen, this is stupid. You're not going to be able to save me.
You can't even get the point of a simple story. How are you
going to know what to say to make me feel better. ... What
would *I like* you to say? Are you seriously asking me to tell
you what you should say to make me feel better? ... What
would be the point? The only reason it would make me feel
better is because you knew enough to say it. ... No, I can't
explain. Look let's drop this now. Ask me something else. ...
Dorothy. What's your name? ... Ken? *(Pause.)* You're going to
have to keep going, Ken. ... I'm fine. That's why I called The
Suicide Center. Just called to say that I'm fine. Now I'm going
to call the morgue and spread the good news. ... Yes, it was a
dumb question. But we're used to that now, aren't we? ... You're
a shrink, aren't you? ... Because shrinks are always doing that.
They're always admitting to you how they don't always know
the right thing to say, and how sometimes they're wrong, and
they make mistakes. They think it gives you confidence to
know that even though your shrink is an asshole he won't lie.
... Oh, do you think that's an interesting thought? That's
interesting. I think it's a dumb thought. ... Okay, let's drop that
now. We're finished with that now. So what are you if you're
not a shrink? ... A para-professional what? ... Yeah, but there
must be an end to the sentence. A para-professional dentist, a
para-professional carrot? What kind of para-professional? ...
Oh, yeah? You do this for your whole living? You don't have
another job in the daytime? ... Well, don't get pissed. I thought
you guys all worked on a volunteer basis like firemen. ... You're
kidding me. Firemen don't work on a volunteer basis? ... Oh,
yeah, of course. ... No, no you're right. The minute you said it
I realized you were right. They're civil service employees. Of

course. They're like cops. It's just that I had this idea in my head... from the movies... some movie I saw when I was a kid... that they were volunteers. Isn't that something? That's really something. Well... I just learned something from you, didn't I? *(There is a brief pause.)* So what do you make at this job? ... That's pretty good if you're only a para-professional. What is a para-professional, exactly? Does that mean you know all about psychology and suicide but they only let you answer the phone? ... Oh, what the fuck are you laughing at with that dumb phoney laugh. That wasn't funny and I didn't mean it to be funny so don't try and make me feel cute. Because I'm not. ... I don't know what's wrong. I just don't feel like getting up anymore. ... In the morning. In the morning, schmuck. When do people get up. ... Well, isn't that enough? I don't feel like getting up anymore and death seems like a good way out of it. ... Nothing happened. Again today nothing happened... I don't know, I guess if everything that happens is just the same as everything else that happens it's the same as nothing happening. ... Well, then it isn't the same. But it feels the same. ... Yes, it's possible that it only feels the same to me. I was who I had in mind. ... Look, don't keep correcting my sentences. I'm not trying to get into college. Do you want to know how I feel or do you want to know how I think I feel from your point of view. ... I feel like shit. ... Because nothing happens. And after nothing happens for long enough you know that this is the nothing that's going to happen to you for the rest of your life so why stay around and watch it. Especially if you feel as bad as I do all the time. ... No, I don't think it's sophisticated. I think it's true. ... Sophistical? Sorry. Hey, are you really this dumb or is this some new kind of technique to see how fast I'll crack. ... Yes, I sound angry. I went through hell to get this number and every time you open your mouth you say something so dumb I'm embarrassed to be talking to you. And I waited until the last minute to call you, too, because I didn't want to use up my last chance. So, naturally, now that you turn out to be this half-wit I'm angry. ... Well, don't apologize. You're doing the best you can. I didn't believe that for the first ten minutes but you've finally convinced me. ... Well, I'm sorry, too. ... No, I'm not. I'm a hooker, sort of. I'm kind of a para-professional. ... Don't do it. I know it sounds like the perfect opening but if you give me the hot line chuckle again I swear to God I'll strangle myself with the telephone cord. ... Thank you. *(Suddenly, nervously.)* Hey, am I keeping you on the phone? You must have a lot of other calls. Is this alright? To talk this long? ... Oh, okay. ... Well, I'm just too disorganized. If someone gives me a number where I can contact them I write it on a napkin or a kleenex and then throw it out. Or I write it on the wall and forget to put the name next to it. And I can't set a price. I just can't decide what a good price is. I want something high enough to be classy but not so high it's discouraging. And I let some guy I picked up in a bar the other night give me a check. I didn't even ask to see his identification. And when I looked at it it was no good. ... I didn't look at it until two days later. ... Because I couldn't make it to the dresser. Sometimes I don't have enough to pay my rent and it's all because I don't have any system. ... Yeah, I'm happy with what I do. It's better than answering the phone all night in a suicide center. It's just that I can't handle the paperwork. I have practically no records. That's a catastrophe in a business like this. ... They're all okay. I don't remember them well enough to have a favorite. ... Oh, I guess I'm good enough. But I know I'll never be great. And I'm very bad at small talk, so that's a drawback. ... I say as little as possible. "Hello" maybe when they come in and "so long" when they leave. ... No, I don't have that problem with my friends. I don't have any friends. ... Because I'm unpleasant. Surely you must have noticed that during the course of our conversation. Why should anyone want to be my friend? Would you want to be my friend? How would you like to spend an evening like this if you weren't on the hot line. Can you see yourself picking up the phone and saying "I guess I'll call Dorothy just for the fun of it". ... Bullshit. Why should you? Who in their right mind would put up with this crap if it wasn't their job. ... See past what? ... This *is* what I'm like. ... Yes. Always. I'm a little nicer tonight because I need you but that could change in a second if you say the wrong thing. ... Yes, I've "sought help". ... It didn't do any good. He was okay. He never said anything much. Maybe "hello" when I came in and "so long" when I left. Sometimes he would say "see you next week" but then I didn't show up. ... Why should he be so fucking sure I was going to show up next week? I was the one who was paying. ... You see? You see what? ... You're full of shit. I don't mean anything. And you don't see anything. I haven't told you the truth in ten minutes. And even that's a lie. And what do you care? You know no matter what I tell you, when I hang up you'll tell the guy sitting next to you that I hate men. ... Because that's what all you guys say. And you're not smart enough to be different. Christ, how smart can you be if you do night work in a suicide center. ... Listen, I'm not having as good a time as I was when we started talking. Maybe seeing you would help. Could you come over? ... Well, I'm an emergency. ... No, I don't want to see someone else. I want to see you. If there's somebody else free to come over, let him answer the phone. I'm sure he can master the technique. *(A*

pause.) So are you coming over? ... Not even to save my life?
... Yeah, but all the other calls are speculation. I'm telling you
you can save me. ... No, later won't count. I want to see you
now. It won't mean anything to me to see you if you don't drop
your hot line and come over now. ... Okay, listen, forget it. ...
Really. Don't get upset. I know you can't come over. I just
asked out of politeness. I'm not going to kill myself over it. ...
No, I don't want to keep talking to you. You can't help me and
there's nothing to say. You just want me to keep talking because
that's what they teach you at The Suicide Center phone school.
"Just keep 'em talking," right? "It doesn't matter what they say
so long as they don't hang up." Right? Have I got it? ... What
are you doing? Thinking about whether or not to tell me if I'm
right? Don't bother I know just how it works. I saw it in a
movie with Sidney Poitier. I know the whole training manual.
And I know that when you hang up on a failure you tell those
you feel closest to that you screwed up. "I kept her on the
phone for forty minutes but I couldn't get her name and
address". How dare you discuss me with anyone else.

*(The lights have come up on KEN L and the left panel has
    opened.)*

KEN. I won't! I won't!
DOROTHY. Yes, you will. And you'll talk it over with your
immediate superior, the actual professional, and ask him what
you said wrong. And he'll tell you that there's never a right
and a wrong thing to say. You just have to feel your way and
hope for the best. Your job is to save lives. But you can't be
arrogant enough to think you can save them all. How dare you
think of me as a life you didn't save. I just called to tell you

that the movie stank and Sidney Poitier was no better than
you are and I think your whole organization is impersonal and
full of shit. And I lied to you.

KEN. Just now?

DOROTHY. No, the last lie. I *am* going to kill myself when
I hang up and if you'd have said you'd come over I wouldn't
have done it. It would have changed everything. You could
have surprised me. I would have stayed alive for another ten
or twenty years because, after all, if there's one surprise maybe
there's another. And you wouldn't even have had to come over.
If you'd have said you wanted to I would have let you off the
hook.

KEN. Dorothy, please... won't you let me keep talking to
you?

DOROTHY. No. You're not interested in me. You're just
interested in keeping me alive. Who the fuck are you to keep
anyone alive? Who the fuck are you anyway. You're a para-
person working at a para-suicide center. And you have just
personally cost me my life. You have failed not because you
couldn't succeed, but because you weren't on your toes. Another cup of coffee, a few hours more sleep and I could've
gone to the movies tomorrow. So think about that tonight, killer.

(DOROTHY hangs up. KEN stares at the phone.)

KEN. Dorothy? *Dorothy?*

*(Without hanging up he quickly picks up the 2nd phone and
    dials "0". DOROTHY picks up the bowl with the pills in it
    and begins swallowing them, one after another.)*

KEN. *(Into phone.)* Operator, this is an emergency. Get me the police! ... No, no, don't give me the number! Connect me with the police! ... I don't know my precinct. ... Operator, I'm reporting a murder! ... I *know* it's 911 but can't you... fuck it, I'll dial it myself. *(He slams the 2nd phone down.)* You idiot.

(Still without hanging up the 1st phone KEN picks up the 2nd phone again and dials 911. MARTY walks in and sees him holding both phones.)

MARTY. Got two? I'll take one. Never take two calls at the same time.

(MARTY reaches for the first phone. KEN leaps back.)

KEN. No! I... a suicidal woman just hung up on me. I'm trying to trace the call. I don't want to break the connection.

MARTY. Well, if she hung up on you the connection's broken.

KEN. Yes, but... it might be easier to trace if... if both of us haven't hung up. ... Oh, *God*!...

MARTY. I can hear the dial tone from here.

KEN. I don't believe this. The Police Emergency number has been ringing for three minutes. I could be dead by now. I could have killed someone by now. I probably *have* killed someone by now.

MARTY. Ken, hang up the other phone. You're tying up a line.

KEN. *(He slams the 1st phone down.)* Oh, shit! That's right. What if she calls back and my line is busy? It will ring at another table.

MARTY. Right.

KEN. Will you please inform everyone in the room that if a woman calls they're to find out if her name is Dorothy and then notify me immediately.

MARTY. Doesn't she know your name?

KEN. Yes, but she may not ask for me. She may not want to talk to me.

MARTY. Well, then... what's the problem? Whoever gets her will handle it...

KEN. *(Grabbing him by the shirt.)* She's going to kill herself, don't you understand? I'm the only one who knows how to prevent it. I don't care who else she talks to . *I'm* the only one who knows what to say to her to keep her alive.

(The phone rings. KEN releases MARTY and snatches it up.)

KEN. Hot... Suicide Center. ... Dorothy? ... Hold on. *(To MARTY.)* How do I switch this call to another table?

MARTY. You can't after you pick up.

KEN. *(Into phone.)* I'm sorry, Miss. I'm expecting an emergency call on this number. Can you call back?

MARTY. Are you crazy? *(He snatches the phone away.)* Hot line.

KEN. *(Trying to grab the phone back.)* No! You've got to clear that line. Dorothy will call on that line.

MARTY. *(Fending him off; into phone.)* ... What's wrong, Glenda?

KEN. *(Raising his voice.)* If anyone here receives a call from Dorothy, please notify me at once. Do you hear? *(Suddenly speaking into the phone he is holding.)* Well, it's about time! Do you realize I've been ringing this number for five minutes to report a police emergency and no one...

(KEN breaks off: listens.)

MARTY. *(Into phone.)* ... You must feel terrible, Glenda...

KEN. *(Into phone.)* My name is Kenneth Gardner. I'm a counselor at the Downtown Suicide Center---666-0066. I need immediate help with a case. Please call as soon as someone is available. *(He slams the phone down.)* This is unbelievable. They have an answerphone at police emergency.

MARTY. *(Into phone.)* ... You must feel very helpless, Glenda...

(The 2nd phone rings. KEN snatches it up.)

KEN. *(Into phone.)* Downtown Suicide Center.

MARTY. *(Into phone.)* ... Well, maybe he was upset, too, Glenda...

KEN. *(Into phone.)* Sir, can you call back...

MARTY. *(Covering his mouthpiece; to KEN.)* No! You can't!

KEN. *(Covering his mouthpiece.)* Please! I have to keep this phone free...

MARTY. You can *not* ask a potential suicide to call back later. How many people do you want to kill tonight?

(DOROTHY begins to nod stage R.)

KEN. *(After a moment; into phone.)* Hello?... Sorry, sir. We're ... we were having a little trouble with this line, but it's alright now. ... Yes, I want very much to talk to you, Mark. What seems to be the trouble? *(Covering mouthpiece; to MARTY.)* Get off that line. Free that line. That's my line. Take that call on your own line. *(Into phone.)* ... I see. That must have been very painful...

MARTY. *(Into phone.)* ... Yes, that's a very bad feeling...

KEN. *(Covering mouthpiece; to MARTY.)* Get off that line before I disconnect you.

(He poises his hand over the 2nd phone.)

MARTY. *(Into phone.)* What's your number, Glenda?

MARTY. *(Into phone.)* Alright, Glenda, you hang in there. I'm going to call you back in one minute. *(He hangs up; to KEN.)* You're psychotic. And I'm reporting you to Russell now!

(MARTY rushes off.)

KEN. *(Into phone.)* ... uh-huh. I see. ... Do you have a family, Mark? *(He stares at the 2nd phone in agony.)* ... I see. How many children? *(The 2nd phone rings. KEN presses the receiver he is holding against his chest and answers it. Softly.)* Hello? *(He glances around.)* Uh... what number are you calling? ... Oh, well, you've got the wrong number. This is a private residence. Try again. You probably misdialed. *(Into 1st phone.)* ... Yes, a depressed person can be a burden, but have you considered how painful it will be for them if you commit suicide, Mark? They'll blame themselves perhaps for the rest of their lives. ... I don't think you *can* take care of it in a note. *(Staring at 2nd phone; under his breath.)* Oh, please. Dorothy, please! *(Into 1st phone.)* ... Well, why not try and talk through it, Mark... *(DOROTHY has now crawled to the phone and dialed a number and waits as it rings.)* ... What is it that seems so hopeless? ... I see. How sick? ... Terminally. ... Uh-huh. ...

Well, Sloan Kettering is an excellent hospital. ... Really? How long a waiting list? ... That long. ... No, I don't know of any oncologists attached to free standing clinics in this city, but why don't I check into this for you? I could call you back or you could call me back. ... My name is Ken. Absolutely. ... Give me until tomorrow. ... Good, because fine work is being done in that field. ... No, no. Crying is not a bad thing. You go ahead and cry. ... No, I'll wait. I'll be right here on the other end of the line for as long as you cry.

(KEN puts his hand over his face and sits listening.)

DOROTHY. *(Into phone.)* This is Miss Duval... box 7... 2... 5. Are there any messages for me?

KEN. *(Into phone.)* Oh! my. Oh! my, my, my. You must feel so bad.

DOROTHY. ... Nothing? Oh. Okay...

(DOROTHY'S head droops. The phone falls.)

KEN. *(Into phone.)* ... Yes, I'm here, Mark.

(DR. RUSSELL comes up behind him, sees he is on the phone and stands watching.)

KEN. ... Good. Now you hold on to that feeling and I'm going to get to work on this right away. ... You bet there's hope. ... I'll talk to you tomorrow night, Mark.

(KEN hangs up. DR. RUSSELL steps forward.)

DR. RUSSELL. I hear you've been having some trouble, Ken.

KEN. Yes. I have a cancer patient, no money, three children, he's on the waiting list for Sloan Kettering but, of course, since they've only given him six months to live he's nervous about time. Can we do anything for him?

DR. RUSSELL. Well, that's out of our province, Ken. But what we *can* do is get him in touch with Cancer Patients Anonymous which provides free counseling to terminal cancer patients.

KEN. I think he was hoping for something more... positive. He seems to want to live.

DR. RUSSELL. Well, in that case, there's nothing we can do for him. Is this the caller Marty told me about... who hung up on you?

KEN. No. She called earlier and asked me to come over and save her and I said I couldn't because I had to man the phones. When she hung up she called me killer.

DR. RUSSELL. *(Gently.)* You must feel enraged, Ken.

KEN. Yes.

DR. RUSSELL. And helpless.

KEN. Yes.

DR. RUSSELL. I think you have to remember, Ken, that potential suicides are potential killers. And if you let them change places with you they'll make you as powerless and impotent as they are.

KEN. I wasn't powerless. I had a choice. I could have gone over.

DR. RUSSELL. And saved her.

KEN. Yes.

DR. RUSSELL. Ken, that is *so* arrogant...

KEN. Please, don't say that to me again, Dr. Russell. I don't want to hear that anymore. Either we're answering these phones because we think it makes a difference--in which case we're arrogant--or we're answering these phones because it makes us feel nice--and that's really arrogant...

DR. RUSSELL. Don't tell me my motives! I'm not the villain here!

KEN. I know that. I'm sorry...

DOROTHY. *(Her head snaps up.)* My note!

KEN. ... I just want you to help me. Please! Just find out if a woman named Dorothy ever called here before. She's a hooker...

(As KEN speaks DOROTHY reaches over, picks up a pencil and paper, and begins laboriously writing.)

DR. RUSSELL. We get hundreds of calls...

KEN. Whoever talked to her will remember her. She's got a vicious tongue and she aims for the balls.

DR. RUSSELL. I'm beginning to understand why you're so frantic, Ken. You must have felt so angry when you talked to her that, unconsciously, you wanted her...

KEN. I didn't want her to die. I still don't want her to die. That's why I'm frantic. Why is that so hard to understand for people who work in a suicide center.

(The phone rings. KEN grabs it.)

KEN. *(Into phone.)* Hello?

DR. RUSSELL. Always answer with "Hot Line", Ken.

KEN. *(To RUSSELL.)* Shut up. *(Into phone.)* ... Yes, this is

Mr. Gardner. The emergency is a potential suicide victim named Dorothy. ... No. No last name. ... Yes, I understand you can't ... please let me finish. She informed me that she got the number of this particular suicide center from Police Emergency. She called Police Emergency specifically for that purpose. So will you please ask everyone who was on the board or taking messages off the answerphone if they spoke to a woman asking for that information. ... Yes, and please hurry. This is urgent.

(DOROTHY stops printing her note, picks up the phone again, dials, and sits waiting as it rings.)

DR. RUSSELL. Ken, I'm going to allow you to finish this, but I don't want you to take any new calls.

KEN. *(Into phone.)* ... Yes? ... I just spoke to someone regarding the nature of my emergency. ... May I ask who I'm speaking to now? .. Sergeant Dryer? ... Sergeant, I'm a little unnerved by your asking me the nature of my emergency after I've just spent five minutes explaining it to another officer. Is this just confusion about which calls have been answered or is it possible that whoever I spoke to has just forgotten about me. ... Thank you. I'm very relieved. It's about a bomb that's been allegedly planted at Police Emergency. ... No, that's alright. I've already given the details to the officer who called me back so, as you just said, why worry.

DR. RUSSELL. You didn't tell me this, Ken. My God I didn't know...

KEN. *(Into phone.)* ... Yes, I'll hold. That's what I was doing when you got on the line.

DR. RUSSELL. Ken, I... didn't understand the nature of this call. You didn't tell me this woman was psychotic.

KEN. *(To RUSSELL.)* Well, now that you understand I would appreciate it if you'd try and get the information I asked for. Dorothy. Hooker. Vicious tongue.

DR. RUSSELL. Right.

(RUSSELL hurries off. KEN sits waiting. DOROTHY sits holding the phone. Her eyelids droop, then snap open.)

DOROTHY. *(Into phone; thickly.)* Hi, I'm calling to find out the name of the officer I spoke to earlier who gave me the name of a Sidney Poitier movie. ... It *is* an emergency...

KEN. *(Into phone.)* ... Yes. Still holding.

DOROTHY. *(Into phone.)* ... I need his name. I promised to thank him in my note and I don't know his name. *(She begins to cry.)* I didn't even ask his name.

KEN. *(Into phone.)* ... I'm holding for Sergeant Dryer...

DOROTHY. *(Into phone.)* ... No I don't want to give you my name. I want his name. He's the only name I have in my note and I don't know it.

KEN. *(Into phone.)* ... Hello, Sergeant Dryer. Yes?

DOROTHY. *(Into phone.)* ... Yes, but I'll only hold for 30 seconds... because I don't want you to trace this call. 1-1000...

KEN. *(Into phone.)* ... That's why I'm trying to find her, Sergeant. She's a potential suicide who claims she's planted several bombs around the city, some at Police Emergency and others in the private homes of specific policemen.

DOROTHY. *(Counting the seconds.)* ... 5-1000... 6-1000...

KEN. *(Into phone.)* ... From my experience as a Hot Line Counselor I don't think it was idle boasting. ... Yes, if we can locate her I'm pretty sure I can get it out of her, but not if she commits suicide first.

DOROTHY. ... 0-1000...
KEN. *(Into phone.)* ... Right.
DOROTHY. ... 10-1000...
KEN. *(Into phone.)* ... Good.
DOROTHY. ... 11-1000
KEN. *(Into phone.)* ... Keep checking.

(MARTY enters. DOROTHY continues to count, softly, her body rocking, rhythmically, her voice fading in and out during the scene.)

MARTY. Ken, I'm really sorry. I didn't know.

(DR. RUSSELL runs in.)

DR. RUSSELL. No luck! No one remembers her.
DOROTHY. ... 13-1000... 14-1000...
KEN. *(Into phone.)* ... Yes, this is Mr. Gardner. ... Yes, Officer Purdy. ... Let's hear it. ... What time was that? ... Yes, that would be about the right time. ... Yes! That's her! ... Definitely. She mentioned the Poitier movie to me, too.
DR. RUSSELL. They should start evacuating the emergency center...
KEN. *Now*? Is he talking to her now? ... Well, put him the fuck on with her before the thirty seconds are up. ... No, don't mention the bombs. I'll handle the bombs. Just get him on before she hangs up. ... Are you tracing it now? ... How long does it take? ... That long? ... Tell him to talk to her about... anything. Tell him to spell out his name, tell him to make up a middle name, tell him to spell out his rank and precinct. ... Is there some way you can tie me into the line so I can talk to

her? I think I can get her name and address. I know what to say now. ... Yes, but it's my specialty. I've been doing it for years. ... Right. *(Without hanging up, he picks up the 2nd phone and dials; then speaks into 1st phone.)* Okay it's ringing.

DOROTHY. *(Her breathing is labored.)* ... 21-1000... 22-1000...

KEN. (Into 2nd phone.) Operator, I've been instructed by the police to call you and... ... You are? *(Into 1st phone.)* The operator says she's talking to you. ... Right.

DR. RUSSELL. What's happening? Have they tied you into her line yet?

KEN. Not yet.

MARTY. What are they doing?

KEN. I don't know. Hello? Hello? Hello! Goddamit!

DOROTHY. 25-1000... 26-1000... 27-1000... *(KEN suddenly hears her and they speak, simultaneously.)* ...28-1000...

KEN. *(Overlapping.)* ... 28-1000... Hello!

(DOROTHY stares at the phone.)

DOROTHY. Hello...?

KEN. Hello! Dorothy? This is Ken. *Surprise!*

DOROTHY. Ken...

KEN. Tell me where you live, Dorothy. I'm coming over.

DOROTHY. I can't ...

KEN. You fucking tell me where you live! I found you. You owe me another twenty years of your life. Because if there's one surprise, maybe there's another. Now tell me where you live.

DOROTHY. *(With great effort.)* ... 120 ... 26th street...

KEN. East or West? Dorothy? East or West?

DOROTHY. East...

(DOROTHY'S head droops.)

KEN. Alright now listen to me. *(He shouts.)* Listen to me!
DOROTHY. *(Her head jerks up.)* East...
KEN. Do you have coffee? Dorothy?
DOROTHY. *(She looks over at the cardboard container from the Burger Shop.)* S'too far...
KEN. You can reach it.
DOROTHY. S'too far...
KEN. Do it, Dorothy. Just *do* it. And I'll keep talking. I'll talk very loud so you can hear me.

(She begins crawling toward the coffee container as KEN continues to talk.)

KEN. *(Raising his voice.)* My name is Ken Gardner and I'm sitting here talking to you, and I'm going to keep on talking to you for as long as it takes because I found you, I *found* you...

(As KEN speaks DOROTHY'S hand reaches the coffee container. The lights begin to fade and the voices of the other counselor's come up over KEN'S.)

1ST VOICE. "You sound very upset, Paul. What's wrong?
2ND VOICE. "Hot line. ... I see. Why don't you tell me what's wrong?"
3RD VOICE. "Hot line. ... Yes, I am. ... Well, that's what I'm here for. Tell me about it..."

END OF PLAY

COSTUME PLOT

DR. RUSSELL
Repeat pants, shirt, socks, shoes, watch
Gray cardigan
Bowtie

KEN
Smallcheck button-down shirt, sleeves rolled
Diagonal striped tie pre-tied
Black plastic watch

MARTY
T-shirt (underall)
Gray corduroy pants, Black leather belt
Gray socks, black hush puppies
Gray sweater or gray shirt w/cardigan sweater
Gray and black wristwatch

DELIVERY MAN:
Gray jeans
Athletic t-shirts
Gray striped shirt, Gray sweatshirt
Gray athletic socks, Black workshoes
Apron
Gray baseball cap
Brown leather jacket

DOROTHY
Balck leotard
Gray striped leggings
Blue sweater w/big collar
Beigel guess wallet
Black suede purse
Earrings

PROPERTY PLOT

On Stage Table
2 Chairs
2 Phones
1 8 1/2 x 11 Pad
1 Pencil

Back Room Table - Off Left Room
1 Folding Chair
1 Red Phone
1 8 1/2 x 11 Pad
1 Pencil
1 Mug: MARTY - with water
1 Mug: DR. RUSSELL - with water
1 Mug: KEN - with water
Sandwich in wax paper & Banana Off Left

Wall Unit
Tissue Box
People Magazine on top shelf
Black Bag with Wallet/Money
　　　Wallet: $4.00 in singles
　　　# 1: 3 Dimes, 1 Nickel, 1 Quarter
　　　# 2: 3 Quarters, 2 Nickels
　　　Black Bag: All Left Over Coins
Lip Stick and Hair Brush
Telephone
Note Pad - Leaning against SR wall of unit
3 Pencils - in cosmetics basket
Arm Chair with throw and Hand Mirror

<u>Ottoman with Radio</u>

<u>Side Table</u>
    1 Pill bottle with 30 pills
    1 Water bottle
    Green glass with sip of water
    Clean Glass bowl

<u>Wall Table</u>
    Lamp

<u>Cardboard Tray Off Right</u>
    Styrofoam Burger Box & Coffee Cup
    White Bag

<u>Coffee Can w/Coins Off Right</u>
    9 Pennies, 6 Quarters, 2 Nickels, 1 Dime

NOTE: CHECK ART WORK ON WALLS

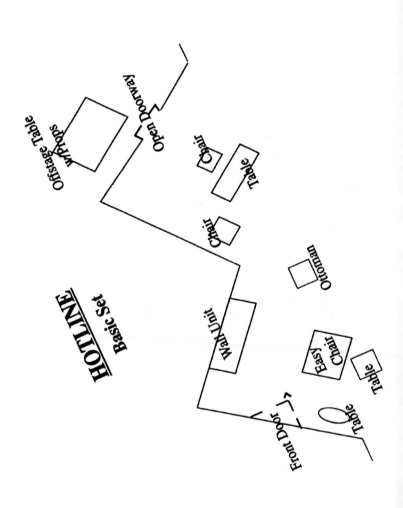

HOTLINE
Basic Set

Offstage Table
w/Props

Open Doorway

Chair

Table

Chair

Ottoman

Wall Unit

Easy
Chair

Table

Front Door

Table

HOTLINE

Stage Right Set up

Wall Unit

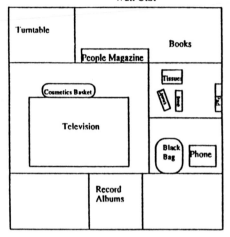

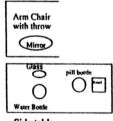

Side table

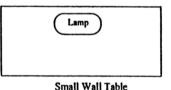

Small Wall Table

HOTLINE

Stage Left Set up

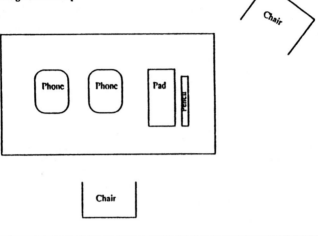

Off Stage Left Room Set up

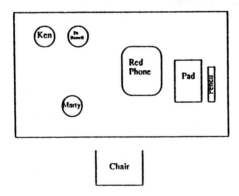

Mugs: Fill with water

CENTRAL PARK WEST

by

Woody Allen

CENTRAL PARK WEST

(It is about 6:00 PM on a November Saturday. No one is on stage as we hear ringing at the door and receiving no response, knocking. This continues throughout.)

CAROL. *(Off stage.)* Phyllis? Phyllis? Phyllis?! Phyllis, are you in there?

(PHYLLIS enters from SR. She sits on the SR end of the sofa.)

CAROL. *(Off stage.)* Phyllis! It's Carol.
PHYLLIS. I'm coming.
CAROL. Are you ok?
PHYLLIS. I'm soaking wet. Caught me in the shower.

(PHYLLIS crosses US to bar. Pours a drink. Downs it. More door buzzing and knocking from CAROL.)

CAROL. Phyllis! Please open the door. Come on, honey!
PHYLLIS. All right. I'm dressed.

(PHYLLIS crosses US to front door and opens it to let CAROL in.)

CAROL. Are you all right?
PHYLLIS. No details, please.

71

CAROL. No details of what?

PHYLLIS. I *said* let's not get into it.

CAROL. Is everyone ok?

PHYLLIS. There are no shadows on anybody's X-rays, if that's what you mean.

CAROL. What X-rays? Who got X-rayed?

PHYLLIS. Why would anyone get X-rayed?

CAROL. What do you mean no shadows?

PHYLLIS. My God--you're so literal--it's such a curse to be literal. A waste of wit--all my jokes and little ironies go straight down the toilet.

CAROL. What is going on?

PHYLLIS. The reference to X-rays implies only that cancer is not responsible for the discovered lump in this tragedy.

CAROL. What tragedy?

PHYLLIS. Please--I'd hardly call this a tragedy.

CAROL. How long have you been drinking?

PHYLLIS. I'm not drunk. It takes a lot more than a little red wine to ring *my* bell. What's the difference between sushi and pussy?

CAROL. Oh, Phyllis—

PHYLLIS. Rice. One of my patients told it to me. Don't try and deconstruct it, Carol--it's a joke, a witticism, a snapper.

CAROL. I'll make some coffee.

PHYLLIS. Only if *you* want it. I'm content to stay with my Chateau-Absolut.

CAROL. What has happened?

PHYLLIS. Same patient who told me the joke referred to his wife's vagina as a bearded clam. He has a little hostility problem with women. His mother was a meter maid.

CAROL. What is the emergency?

PHYLLIS. What emergency?

CAROL. The message on my service.

PHYLLIS. *(Noticing her garment.)* Where'd you get that?

CAROL. That what?

PHYLLIS. Not them there eyes, honey--the coat.

CAROL. This coat?

PHYLLIS. Now you got it.

CAROL. You've seen this coat a hundred times.

PHYLLIS. I have?

CAROL. Including yesterday.

PHYLLIS. One of my patients was wearing this sable coat or lynx--I know they're not in the same family but you get the idea...

CAROL. Phyllis, what is the emergency?

PHYLLIS. And these acned fanatics accosted her right on Fifth Avenue. Those ones who can't bear killing minks--and they started harassing her and then some of the anti-vivisectionists or whatever they are got physical and they pulled her coat off and underneath she was stark naked.

CAROL. Why?

PHYLLIS. Because she's a whore. She's a high priced whore and I've been treating her for research on my book and she was on an out-call to a guy who wanted a woman to knock on his door in a fur coat and nothing under it. So there she was on Fifth Avenue and Fifty-Seventh Street and everybody saw her bearded clam.

CAROL. Is Sam all right?

PHYLLIS. No details, please.

CAROL. Is he?

PHYLLIS. He's fine. You know Sam--he does a hundred push-ups in the time it takes me to floss two teeth.

CAROL. And the boys?

PHYLLIS. Away--away down south in the land of cotton—

CAROL. And there's not problem with them at school?

PHYLLIS. They don't cotton to it--and the university doesn't cotton to them... God, there's so much cotton here my mouth is dry.

(PHYLLIS pours a drink.)

CAROL. Why are you so distraught?

PHYLLIS. Distraught? I haven't even reacted yet--this is nothing--you got that? Nothing--nada--zilch--*where'd* you get that coat?

CAROL. Bloomingdale's. Last year.

PHYLLIS. And you wear it a lot?

CAROL. All the time.

PHYLLIS. What animal?

CAROL. It's a good old Republican cloth coat. Now why did you leave that hysterical message?

PHYLLIS. I'd rather not discuss it.

CAROL. You'd rather not discuss it? I get this frantic, desperate message--emergency, crisis--help. I called you ten times.

PHYLLIS. Was that you?

CAROL. It sure was.

PHYLLIS. Usually I can tell your ring. It's tremulous and tentative.

CAROL. Where is Sam? What is wrong?

PHYLLIS. I don't want to tell you.

CAROL. Why'd you call me?

PHYLLIS. Because I have to talk to someone.

CAROL. So talk.

PHYLLIS. Can we not discuss it?

CAROL. Phyllis—

PHYLLIS. Can't you see I'm being evasive?

CAROL. Why?

PHYLLIS. I'm sorry if I inconvenienced you.

CAROL. You didn't.

PHYLLIS. Did you and Howard have plans?

CAROL. No. I was at Sotheby's

PHYLLIS. What'd you get?

CAROL. Nothing. They were auctioning off baseball cards and Howard wanted to see them and it's the last day.

PHYLLIS. So you two did have plans.

CAROL. No, because Howard couldn't go because today is the day he had to drive his father to Westchester and put him in the home.

PHYLLIS. How sad.

CAROL. He's ninety-three--he's had a good life--or maybe it was a lousy life--but a long one. And he never had any health problems or so they thought except what they didn't know was that he was having a long series of silent strokes. First he started forgetting things, then hearing musical sounds and finally he tried to re-enlist in the army.

PHYLLIS. Howard must be devastated.

CAROL. *(Looking at her watch.)* I left a message for him to meet me here. So. Phyllis, what's going on.

PHYLLIS. Look how she probes.

CAROL. Stop it. You called me.

PHYLLIS. But you always probe--you're always fishing for information.

CAROL. How am I fishing? You call and say it's life an death. I—

PHYLLIS. *(Softly.)* I'm ashamed to tell you what happened, Carol.

CAROL. *(Realizing for the first time the broken statuette.)* Your Nefertiti is broken.

PHYLLIS. My Nefertiti is fine. That's Amenhotep. It's the other sex. For those prices, you'd think they'd throw in a penis.

CAROL. In fact, this whole place looks a little in disarray.

PHYLLIS. Aren't you observant. I, on the other hand, failed to notice that drop dead coat from Bloomingdales' after repeated exposure to it.

CAROL. What'd you do, get robbed?

PHYLLIS. What color is that coat? Puce?

CAROL. No, it's yellow-ish.

PHYLLIS. It's puce.

CAROL. Ok, it's puce.

PHYLLIS. You should never wear puce. It doesn't go with hazel eyes.

CAROL. I don't have hazel eyes.

PHYLLIS. One of them is--the one that looks off that way—

CAROL. Stop being evil, Phyllis. Did you have a fight with Sam?

PHYLLIS. Not exactly—

CAROL. Meaning? God, this is like pulling teeth.

PHYLLIS. Your teeth are good. It was worth every penny.

CAROL. *(Dryly.)* Thank you.

PHYLLIS. The collagen on the other hand...

CAROL. You did not have a fight with Sam?

PHYLLIS. Yes, I did—

CAROL. You said, not exactly—

PHYLLIS. Not exactly what?

CAROL. Not exactly a fight--I just asked if you and Sam had a fight and you said—

PHYLLIS. I did, Sam did not.

CAROL. What did Sam do while you were fighting?

PHYLLIS. He watched me fight.

CAROL. And then?

PHYLLIS. And then he ducked—

CAROL. You hit him?

PHYLLIS. I missed him--if I'd hit him he'd be dead with hieroglyphics on his skull.

CAROL. You threw this statue at Sam? It's heavy.

PHYLLIS I counted on that. Want another drink?

CAROL. Phyllis, what has happened?

PHYLLIS. Oh, Carol--Carol--Carol--Carol--friend Carol.

CAROL. You know, I think I am going to need that drink.

PHYLLIS. He left me.

CAROL. He did?

PHYLLIS. Yes.

CAROL. How do you know?

PHYLLIS. How do I know? How do I know he left me? Because he walked out the door with his belongings and he's getting a divorce.

CAROL. I have to sit down--my legs are weak.

PHYLLIS. You legs are weak?

CAROL. What reason did he give?

PHYLLIS. He doesn't love me anymore--he doesn't like to be around me and he can't stand putting that industrial strength fire hose he keeps behind his fly inside me anymore. Those are the vague reasons he gives but I think he's just being po-lite. I think he really doesn't like my cooking.

CAROL. Out of left field.

PHYLLIS. Well, to me it was out of left field but I'm not perceptive--I'm just an analyst.

CAROL. And he never said anything--or hinted?

PHYLLIS. He never said anything--but that was probably because we never spoke.

CAROL. Well, Phyllis—

PHYLLIS. I mean we spoke--it wasn't just, "pass the salt," although that came up once in a while.

CAROL. But you must have had conversations where he indicated something—

PHYLLIS. Let me put it this way--we both spoke but at the same time. What I mean is, there were two speakers but no listeners.

CAROL. Failure to communicate.

PHYLLIS. God, Carol, how you cut right to the heart of things.

CAROL. Well, it should have told you something.

PHYLLIS. It did.

CAROL. Well, what?

PHYLLIS. I don't know, I wasn't listening, I was talking.

CAROL. And the sex fell off.

PHYLLIS. How did you know?

CAROL. I didn't, I'm assuming.

PHYLLIS. Well, don't assume. People can stop communicating verbally and the sex can still be ferocious.

CAROL. Ok--so the sex was great.

PHYLLIS. Great? It was better than great--it was non-existent.

CAROL. Somewhere along the line the love-making slips away--but that's only because something deeper has already slipped away. Or is it the other way around? The sex goes and

then everything else looses all its luster. The point is--
everything is ephemeral.

PHYLLIS. Is it, Carol?

CAROL. Oh--I don't know--you're asking the wrong person.

PHYLLIS. I don't remember asking.

CAROL. So he didn't say anything other than he was leaving?

PHYLLIS. Like what?

CAROL. Anything?

PHYLLIS. Yeah, he said that even though it wasn't part of
our pre-nuptial agreement, he'd go on paying for my delivery
of the *Sunday Times.*

CAROL. But he did not say where he was going?

PHYLLIS. *(Something setting in.)* I'm beginning to react
to it now.

CAROL. Phyllis, you've been reacting—

PHYLLIS. No--I'm a late reactor... That motherfucker!
Twelve years of marriage and he just ups and walks out! But
he still needs all his papers! And here's what he'll find! Here's
his work!

CAROL. Take it easy!

*(PHYLLIS crosses to SAM'S briefcase on coffee table. Dumps
out the contents and throws the briefcase across the stage.)*

PHYLLIS. *(As she tears up strewn documents.)* We were
just talking about re-doing the house in Amagansett. I said,
we haven't touched it since we first bought it--I said let's get
Paul and Cindi's architect and re-do it all--he said, Phyllis, I
want to talk to you--I said, the house is so well situated on the

bay and we've had such good times there--he said, Phyllis, I don't know how to tell you this but I want out--I didn't hear him--it was one of those conversations where nobody listens--I said, we always wanted picture windows and a bigger bathroom--he said, Phyllis, I'm leaving you--and I said, with one of those showers with many spigots that spray you from all sides--and he grabbed me and said, I don't love you anymore--I want a new life--I want out, I want out, *I want out!* And I said, what color should we paint the guest room?

CAROL. What did he say?

PHYLLIS. Can't you see that I'm humiliated by this--is it that you revel in my humiliation?

CAROL. Phyllis, you don't know what you're saying.

PHYLLIS. He said, I'm in love with another woman.

(CAROL coughs and nearly gags on her drink.)

PHYLLIS. Are you ok? Or do I have to do the Heimlich maneuver?

CAROL. Did he say who she was?

PHYLLIS. I have a patient who gagged on a fish bone at Le Bernadin and a stranger came up behind her and performed the Heimlich maneuver on her and it aroused her--and now wherever she dines, she gags—

CAROL. Did he say who he was leaving you for?

PHYLLIS. Why do you look so uncomfortable?

CAROL. I'm not--I'm just beginning to feel that drink.

PHYLLIS. At first I thought it was Anne Dreyfuss.

CAROL. Anne Dreyfuss? The decorator?

PHYLLIS. She likes all the shit he likes--boating, the woods, skiing—

CAROL. He would never take up with Anne Dreyfuss.

PHYLLIS. How do *you* know?

CAROL. What do you mean, how do I know? I know Sam too.

PHYLLIS. Not as well as me.

CAROL. Well, of course not. I didn't mean that. I just meant that we've all been friends for years

PHYLLIS. How many years?

CAROL. Five--almost six--what has that got to do with anything? I just cannot see Sam with Anne Dreyfuss. She's a whiner--with a very annoying personality and if I may say so, no fanny.

PHYLLIS. I also thought it might be Nonny--the girl in his law firm. She's a partner now...

CAROL. I don't know Nonny--what's she like?

PHYLLIS. Buxom and cute. With an erotic overbite. It's not Nonny.

CAROL. The point is you obviously don't know who he's gone off with.

PHYLLIS. The point is I do. Or at least I think I figured it out.

CAROL. You know, I'm really not feeling very well.

PHYLLIS. Don't tell me you're gonna barf.

CAROL. I can't drink. I always think I can handle it but it just saturates my brain.

PHYLLIS. Your brain? But you only had a thimble full. There's a joke in there somewhere.

CAROL. It's the same with coffee or aspirin. Everything over-stimulates my system. I should never introduce a foreign substance into my body—

PHYLLIS. It's a little late for that.

CAROL. Maybe some coffee...

PHYLLIS. I may have some compazine suppositories. I'd say you're a medium or a large.

(PHYLLIS exits USL.)

CAROL. *(Alone, she secretly picks up the phone, dials.)* Hello? B18--any messages? ... Yes... Howard... what time?... Ok. anything else? *(Tense and interested.)* Yes? Did he say what number he'd be at? What time? Ok, ok...

(CAROL hangs up.)

PHYLLIS. *(Entering from USL.)* I found this Bergdorf's bag so if you suddenly barf it'll be into familiar surroundings. Who'd you call?

CAROL. Call?

PHYLLIS. Yes, the second I left the room you dove for the instrument like you were going down on Cary Grant.

CAROL. Look, I like to check my service because Howard's had a bad day...

PHYLLIS. Can we get back to who my husband left me for?

CAROL. What about my coffee?

PHYLLIS. Know how I figured out who it was?

CAROL. It's none of my business.

PHYLLIS. Sure it is—

CAROL. It's not--I'm sorry it happened--my head is swimming.

PHYLLIS. Know who it is?

CAROL. Please, Phyllis.

PHYLLIS. It's you, you cunt!

CAROL. Oh--the arrant paranoia!

PHYLLIS. Don't give me that, toots--he's been dipping his wick in you for longer that I probably think.

CAROL. You're nuts--get a grip on yourself.

PHYLLIS. You're gonna have to come clean anyway--if you want to go off with him. It's a nice little fillip for Howard-- first dad in the laughing academy and then a dear John letter from the little woman.

CAROL. You know, I am so turned around by this that I can't even respond well.

PHYLLIS. Have you been having an affair with Sam?

CAROL. No.

PHYLLIS. Just tell me.

CAROL. No.

PHYLLIS. I just want the truth.

CAROL. I have not--you're such a bully.

PHYLLIS. I figured it out, harlot. You've been phoning each other, meeting secretly, traveling together—

CAROL. I won't sit here and be accused—

(CAROL rises but still woozy, she sits.)

PHYLLIS. Now--*after* the fact--I remember so many obvious things--the looks across the table--the getting lost together on the trip to Normandy. Howard and I looked for two hours--and the night you ate here and Sam went downstairs to put you in a cab--I'm sitting in bed for an hour and a half while he decided to walk you home--You know, as I speak it's occurring to me that three years ago--three fucking years ago-- you and Sam were in New York for a week with Howard in

L.A. and me at a convention in Philadelphia--that was three years ago or does it go back even further than that?

CAROL. It's not me!

PHYLLIS. I found his Filofax. You're all over it!

CAROL. *(Rises, screams and cries.)* What do you want me to do? We fell in love! You're such a bully!

PHYLLIS. Chrrrrist!

CAROL. Bully! Bully! We fell in love--nobody planned it--nobody wanted to hurt anyone.

PHYLLIS. I knew it--from the night we met the two of you in the Hamptons. I said she's trouble--she's a troubled broad--she reeks from problems--neurosis oozes out of every pore—

CAROL. This affair has caused us nothing but anguish and pain.

PHYLLIS. Don't forget remorse and regret--plus an occasional orgasm.

CAROL. Don't dirty it up--it's not what you think.

PHYLLIS. I said that first night when we drove home--He seems nice--a little lost but decent--but she's borderline and carnivorous.

CAROL. Stop being so judgmental--you know from your work these things happen--it's chemistry--two people meet--and a spark flares up and suddenly it has a life of its own.

PHYLLIS. Stop romanticizing it, you little cooze.

CAROL. It's serious, Phyllis.

PHYLLIS. How long has this been going on? Three years? More? Four? Five?

CAROL. Not even three.

PHYLLIS. So, two? Two years you two have been sneaking around town like dogs in heat?

CAROL. We haven't been sneaking around town--we have an apartment.

PHYLLIS. An apartment? Where?

CAROL. The East Fifties—

PHYLLIS. How big?

CAROL. Small—

PHYLLIS. What?

CAROL. Three rooms.

PHYLLIS. Rent controlled?

CAROL. Stop being snotty--we're trying to communicate—

PHYLLIS. What do you need three rooms for? You entertain?

CAROL. Never. Never. I swear. It's just a place to go to, to be alone--to relax--to--to--to talk—

PHYLLIS. To talk--to exchange ideas.

CAROL. Phyllis, we're in love--oh God--I never thought I'd be saying this--it's--everything--yes, it's sensual, but it's more--we share feelings and dreams.

PHYLLIS. Why did I ever let you into my life--I always know you'd fuck a snake if they held its head.

CAROL. Phyllis, what do you want me to say? He fell out of love with you years ago. I don't know why. Certainly not over me. It was finished in Sam's mind between you two before he ever said anything to me.

PHYLLIS. How did he first do it?

CAROL. Do what?

PHYLLIS. When? What night?

CAROL. What's the difference?

PHYLLIS. You probed--I want answers.

CAROL. New Year's Eve at Lou Stein's party.

PHYLLIS. Oh my God--that was 1992.

CAROL. 93--oh yeah, 92, right...

PHYLLIS. And what happened? Who groped whom first?

CAROL. It wasn't like that. He came over to me--I was watching the fireworks--and he whispered in my ear--can you meet me next week for lunch without mentioning anything to Phyllis. Well, as you can imagine, I was a bit surprised.

PHYLLIS. I'm sure. You probably started to lubricate.

CAROL. I said, why? And he said I need your help on something.

PHYLLIS. And where was I when this adolescent bullshit was going on?

CAROL. You had led a group out onto the terrace, against their will, in the five degree temperature, to watch the fireworks. And Howard was in the kitchen getting the Stein's recipe for Babaganoush.

PHYLLIS. Yes--I remember--your husband had just enrolled in a cooking course and we were all so proud of him.

CAROL. And I said, what kind of help? With what? And Sam said, Phyllis's birthday is soon and I want you to help me get her something but it has got to be something special.

PHYLLIS. And it was, folks.

CAROL. So the following Thursday we met for lunch at his club and we pitched some gift ideas back and forth. And after lunch we went on our shop--I remember going to Bergdorf's and Tiffany's and James Robinson and finally in this tiny old antique store on First Avenue we found a stunning pair of art-deco earrings--diamonds with tiny rubies—

PHYLLIS. I know the earrings. I've seen them on you.

CAROL. Well, I was flabbergasted. He bought them, and we walked out on the street and then he handed the box to me and said, "Here, I want you so badly."

PHYLLIS. And what did you say?

CAROL. I said, whoa--wait a minute--we came to buy

Phyllis a birthday gift--if I take this we have to at least pick out *something* for her.

PHYLLIS. Thanks, you're such a doll. So I wound up with those stinking silver candlesticks.

CAROL. They cost a fortune.

PHYLLIS. They're old lady candlesticks--they're something you'd give Miss Haversham! And of course you never thought to say--Phyllis is your wife and I'm her friend—

CAROL. May I tell you why not—

PHYLLIS. I know why not, you cheap little tart--because you had your predatory sights set on Sam from the minute you met him.

CAROL. Not so—

PHYLLIS. Don't give me that shit--you met us and took one look at him and started rubbing your hands together and salivating because he works for a show business law firm and he's in shape and has muscles and compared to that emasculated, goat-turd of a husband you have, Sam must seem like the answer to a bovine frump's prayer.

CAROL. He couldn't stand being married to you anymore and he told me that over lunch--*he* initiated the relationship.. he salivated over me--he looked me in the eye at lunch and tears formed--I'm not happy, he said—

PHYLLIS. Tears formed in Sam's eyes? Was his athletic supporter too tight?

CAROL. From the first moment Howard and I met you and Sam I knew he was miserable. This woman is not making him happy--I told that to Howard that first night we met you two—

PHYLLIS. I can see the picture at home--you brushing your former teeth--Howard slipping into his nightgown and

sleeping cap--discussing your betters--planning your little
social climb—

CAROL. She may be a brilliant shrink and the center of
every conversation with some new variation of how great she
is--but she's not enough woman for him--she's not there to
guide him--to bring him coffee—

PHYLLIS. Can you pass me that airsick bag?

CAROL. Sam had tremendous hostility--but you know that
now.

PHYLLIS. The thought of you and Sam discussing me over
cocktails or post-coital Marlboros.

CAROL. We tried to break it off several times but we
couldn't.

PHYLLIS. I'm sure you tried. But I know Sam--when that
old sperm count rises--you got the phone call--"beat it over here,
honey, I want to get my rocks off and whine about my wife."

CAROL. No, it was not like that--we spoke more often
than made love.

PHYLLIS. About what? Chrrrist, what the hell did he find
to talk about with you? He's a man's man--what the hell did
you have to discuss with him besides me? Your cellulite? Your
eye jobs and chin tucks? Shopping? Your trainer? Your nutritionist? Or did you just lay on his shoulder and giggle about
the ironic shrink who could see everybody's problems but her
own.

CAROL. I did nothing wrong. Your husband stopped lov-
ing you before he met me.

PHYLLIS. Bullshit!

CAROL. And it was obvious to all our friends—

PHYLLIS. They're not our friends--they're my friends. I
brought you in--like a fool--you met them all through me—

CAROL. And they all knew you and Sam were a joke as a couple—

PHYLLIS. Bullshit.

CAROL. Believe me, I did not seduce Sam. He played around plenty before I came on the scene.

PHYLLIS. Like hell!

CAROL. Face up to it!

PHYLLIS. I'm not interested in your fantasies.

CAROL. Ask Edith Moss and Steve Pollack's secretary—

PHYLLIS. Liar! Slut! You're the all-American whore! They should put your diaphragm in the Smithsonian.

CAROL. Don't lay it all on me! I didn't turn your husband into a philanderer—

PHYLLIS. Trollop, tart, prostitute—

CAROL. You're such a phoney--pretending your marriage is so perfect--You were a laughing stock—

PHYLLIS. I loved Sam and I was a damn good wife.

CAROL. We happened to fall in love--but before he met me he was groping several of your closest high class friends--including Madelaine who also being a shrink probably dissected you with far greater insight than I'm capable of.

PHYLLIS. Madelaine is the kind of shrink who has no insights--she uses tarot cards.

(Door buzzer rings. PHYLLIS gets it. It's HOWARD.)

HOWARD. What a day--oh brother--I need a drink.

PHYLLIS. Howard, guess what?

CAROL. Will you keep quiet.

HOWARD. *(Pouring himself a drink.)* You look at them in that home and you realize that's what it all comes to--to that--

to that. My God--what's the point of anything if it ends up like that--

PHYLLIS. Carol has some news for you that might cheer you up.

CAROL. Will you stop--Howard, she's drunk.

HOWARD. *(Going for drink.)* I mean to get good and drunk tonight. God, Carol--here's my father who was a strapping, virile man--he took me to ball games.

PHYLLIS. Tell him, Carol--he needs a lift.

HOWARD. This poor old lady, ninety-one, used to be a singer--sits at the piano--she's ancient--trying to gasp her way through a chorus of "You're The Cream In My Coffee"... the others stare--some perfunctory applause--and these living dead seated in stupors before the communal TV, their clothes stained from food that dribbles all over them...

PHYLLIS. I hope you reserved us all a place--

HOWARD. I can't bear it! It's too much to bear!

CAROL. Have your drink--

HOWARD. Two people grow old together--like my mother and father--we decay--one of us breaks down faster--the other watches--after years of being together--suddenly you're alone--

PHYLLIS. It may not happen quite that way for you, Howard--

HOWARD. No... *(To himself.)* It might not.

PHYLLIS. Tell him, Carol--

HOWARD. Tell me what? What's going on? Why are you drunk so early? And what the hell's all this?

(HOWARD is noticing the mess for the first time.)

CAROL. Howard, there's something we need to discuss—

HOWARD. What?

CAROL. I'm not sure this is the time or place.

PHYLLIS. Howard, Carol's leaving you.

CAROL. Will you let us be—

HOWARD. I don't get it.

PHYLLIS. She's leaving you--she's going off with another man.

HOWARD. Meaning what?

PHYLLIS. Meaning you're out--no more wifekins--she's been fucking my husband for three years and she's going off with him.

CAROL. *(To PHYLLIS.)* You're detestable.

PHYLLIS. Am I lying? Close your mouth, Howard.

HOWARD. Is this true, Carol?

CAROL. Sam and I fell in love we didn't mean to hurt anybody.

HOWARD. *(Sitting slowly.)* N-no--I'm sure you didn't...

PHYLLIS. Jesus, aren't you going to get mad?

HOWARD. What's the point? That won't undo things—

PHYLLIS. There's a time to be rational and a time to run amuck--I keep the steak knives in the blue drawer.

(HOWARD drinks.)

HOWARD. *(Not understanding.)* You never had a good word to say about Sam.

PHYLLIS. She was deceiving you, Howard.

CAROL. Will you shut up! You hover around making spiteful remarks--things are bad enough.

HOWARD. *(Simply.)* She was always so jealous of you, Phyllis—

PHYLLIS. Well, she's certainly paid me back.

HOWARD. Sam was my friend—

CAROL. Why do you tell her I'm jealous of her? How was I ever jealous?

HOWARD. It was more than jealously. You were obsessed with her.

CAROL. You're dreaming, Howard.

HOWARD. I'm a writer, Carol--I know how to recognize obsession—

CAROL. You are a failed writer, Howard--they don't recognize things too well--that's why you teach.

HOWARD. You were obsessed with everything about Phyllis.

CAROL. I was not, God damn it!

PHYLLIS. Children, let's not quarrel.

HOWARD. Jesus, Carol, you thought she was an artist. You thought of going back to school to study psychiatry.

PHYLLIS. So the truth comes out--hero worship.

CAROL. Stop drinking, Howard, you're worse than me.

HOWARD. I can drink--you're the one who makes a spectacle--She used to dress like you--remember? And you wanted to cut your hair—

PHYLLIS. This is becoming positively morbid.

CAROL. I was always fascinated by psychiatry. I minored in it in college.

HOWARD. You minored in history.

PHYLLIS. I thought it was art.

CAROL. I was an art history major.

PHYLLIS. You were a shopping major.

HOWARD. She likes to say she hasn't found herself.

PHYLLIS. Has she tried looking in the reptile house?

CAROL. *(Explaining rationally.)* There was a period of time that I was very impressed by you.

HOWARD. And she talked of becoming a shrink.

PHYLLIS. Fortunately they have licensing laws—

HOWARD. She was going to combine it with her yoga--an Eastern religion psychotherapy. An Eastern religious, holistic, nutritionist, waking dream therapy.

PHYLLIS. Where were you going to practice--in Calcutta or the East Village?

CAROL. Go ahead--make fun of me.

HOWARD. And for a while she dressed like you--she ordered all those simple skirts and tops--I remember on more than one occasion you rejected an outfit because you said Phyllis Riggs would never wear anything like that.

CAROL. He makes this up. Howard, your father's dying, don't take it out on me.

HOWARD. Carol's always had an identity problem. She doesn't know who she is. Or rather she knows who she is and she's desperately trying to find someone else to be --and who can blame her.

CAROL. All right, calm down. I think you're overdue for your treatments. Howard's mood swings have been getting much worse lately. He doesn't like it known.

HOWARD. Don't change the subject.

CAROL. Now he's joined the Hemlock Society. That's what I've had to put up with all these years. That kind of mentality.

PHYLLIS. The Hemlock Society--I hope they made you a lifetime member.

CAROL. Every now and then when things get rough, I notice him eyeing the Baggies--that's the method of choice for the society--a plastic bag on the head.

HOWARD. I'm not going to wind up in one of those homes, I'll tell you that.

CAROL. And then just as quickly he'll become happy--too happy.

HOWARD. Quiet, Carol.

CAROL. God, if you think I shop--when Howard swings into his uphill phase--he just checks into the Plaza and runs up all kinds of bills--champagne and caviar and things he'll never wear--and big plans and grandiose schemes--and the only thing that straightens him out is electricity. This man needs his voltage like we need our mixed green salads. And he begs me to hide it.

HOWARD. At least I have an identity. I'm Howard who's manic-depressive. Carol wants to be you but you're already taken—

PHYLLIS. So she steals my husband.

HOWARD. It's not just you--she identifies with lots of people.

CAROL. I didn't steal your husband--he came after me.

HOWARD. Her real identity crisis was with her art professor at school. CAROL. Howard, I think we should drop this subject now. I think you and I should go home.

HOWARD. Home? We have no more home.

PHYLLIS. What about her college professor?

CAROL. Howard, I'm warning you—

HOWARD. As long as we're coming clean, you may as well know that when we met, Carol had this art professor--quite a brilliant woman--not with your honors but very impressive...

CAROL. Howard, I will not stay here if you tell this story.

HOWARD. You have no clout with me anymore, Carol--I've been left.

CAROL. You're burning all bridges. Is that what you want?

HOWARD. And Carol grew to idolize this professor and identify with her.

CAROL. Quiet! Quiet!

HOWARD. *(Shaking CAROL.)* Will you shut up!

CAROL. Don't you dare attack me!

HOWARD. Well, don't interrupt me.

PHYLLIS. Howard, you have a temper. I think there's a little bit of the tomboy in you.

HOWARD. She identified with Professor Kanin as much as she identified with you--duplicating her wardrobe--braiding her hair, taking on her mannerisms--reflecting all her tastes-- And because Professor Kanin had a tiny child, Carol decided she wanted to be a mother.

CAROL. I don't care if you tell this story because I can hold my head high.

HOWARD. And so she begged me to make her pregnant-- which I did—

CAROL. With some effort, darling--don't leave out the part about the sudden impotence. Talk about trying to stuff an oyster into a parking meter.

HOWARD. Not that I wanted a child--nor did Carol down deep.

CAROL. You have never known what I felt down deep about anything.

HOWARD. But how else to become Professor Kanin--the idol of the day.

CAROL. You couldn't make me pregnant--is that the story you want to tell? Because that's the long and short of it.

HOWARD. She visited a fertility expert--and every few days I'd be asked to masturbate into a test tube—

PHYLLIS. My God, what an aim you must have had.

HOWARD. So she could run with it in a taxi cab and while the sperm were still fresh and squiggling—

CAROL. Yours did not squiggle, Howard, they wandered aimlessly—

HOWARD. To make a long story short--science worked its magic and she got knocked up. Her dream was going to come true. In nine months she would be just like Professor Kanin--with her Laura Ashley skirts and the Aztec jewelry--art major, mother, the works--she wouldn't have to go on being the unenviable character Carol.

PHYLLIS. I can see this coming--she got cold feet and eighty-sixed the fetus.

HOWARD. No--well, yes--but she got cold feet in her eighth month--so to get rid of the blessed event then would be messy if not totally impossible. But suddenly she didn't want to be a mother.

CAROL. (Softly.) No--I didn't.

HOWARD. Reality set in and she said to herself, "Hey, it's one thing to have fantasies of identification--but I'm not Professor Kanin and I don't want a child."

CAROL. Why are you doing this?

HOWARD. So she dropped her foal--our foal--or hers, mine, and the fertility expert's--I should give him a collaborators credit.

CAROL. (Crying.) He was a baby--so tiny—

HOWARD. And I thought he was rather cute considering all the blood and tears. He looked a little like the movie actor Broderick Crawford--but you know they all look like old men. I mean they're bald--and I bonded with him in the first sixty seconds--but darned if she didn't give him away.

PHYLLIS. What a nasty little secret.

HOWARD. She insisted on placing him out for adoption—

PHYLLIS. And you were probably very rational about it. Very sensible and well mannered--reasonable--and then your son was gone.

HOWARD. Yes--gone--I know not where—

PHYLLIS. So somewhere in this vast world is a young man with his father's courage and strength of character and his mother's deep moral integrity. A superman.

CAROL. *(Crying.)* I'm lost... I'm lost...

PHYLLIS. You sure are, baby. And now--I'm going to the toilet and I want you both out of here when I return.

(PHYLLIS exits SL)

HOWARD. So I guess it's over between us.

CAROL. I guess it never should have begun.

HOWARD. Why do you say that, Carol? It certainly began well enough.

CAROL. No--it was my fault. You'd have done better if you had married that what's her name--Ida--Ida—

HOWARD. Rondilino—

CAROL. Rondilino. I should never have taken you away from her--but I wanted to be with a creative soul--a writer—

HOWARD. You didn't take me away from Ida. I saw you and I went after you.

CAROL. That's what you *think*--but the night we all double dated, and I decided I wanted to marry you, you were dead meat.

HOWARD. Poor Ida.

CAROL. Ida was insipid. But better suited to you than I am. Oh Howard, we have disappointed one another too much.

HOWARD. Did you ever cheat on me prior to your affair with Sam?

CAROL. No--Yeah, once. My dentist.

HOWARD. Oh Carol—

CAROL. Oh, Howard--think of it as an extra filling.

HOWARD. Who else?

CAROL. No one... Jay Roland.

HOWARD. My collaborator?

CAROL. Oh, he was such a bad writer, Howard--but sexy with that pony tail.

HOWARD. You slept with my writing partner?

CAROL. Once in his new Mercedes. He wanted to test the shock absorbers.

HOWARD. Who else?

CAROL. No one--that's it--that's it. Those were the years--fifteen arid years--without ever getting up the nerve to leave--betting wrong that all you mental instability was a sure sign of literary genius when in fact it was just plain dementia.

HOWARD. Where will you live?

CAROL. Sam has talked about London.

HOWARD. I don't want you to leave me, Carol.

CAROL. Oh Howard, how can I not? I've become involved with someone who means something to me--something real--there's feelings--there's passion.

HOWARD. I'm a person who can't be alone, Carol.

CAROL. You'll get by--Howard, try and understand, I'm nearly fifty--how many more chances will I get? Now let me go with this guiltlessly.

HOWARD. But I'm scared—

CAROL. Double your prozac--It's a lot better than alcohol, that's for sure. You're just in one of your moods--triggered

by committing your father--and then my news--I say, call
Doctor Carr. I mean if things get really out of hand you can
always go in for a little juice--I--*(She notices HOWARD has
removed a pistol from his pocket.)* Howard--what are you
doing?

HOWARD. I think life is a black hole.

CAROL. Oh my God! Howard--don't!

HOWARD. It's unbearable! I don't want to live.

CAROL. Where did you get that gun?

HOWARD. This was amongst my father's possessions--he
was in the great war--I mean the first great war--the war to
end all wars--only of course it didn't, people being what they
are—

CAROL. Put that down!

HOWARD. It's all so squalid and meaningless!

CAROL. Help! Phyllis! Phyllis!

HOWARD. Shut up, my head is throbbing!

CAROL. Suicide is not the answer!

HOWARD. It all comes to nothing--a void, a home for the
aged.

CAROL. Howard, black moods pass! It's just the moment--
Phyllis! God damn it! Suicide is not the answer.

HOWARD. I'm frightened!

CAROL. Oh God, I can't watch!

HOWARD. You won't have to watch. I'm going to kill you
first--then myself.

CAROL. Me? Howard, you're joking!

HOWARD. First you, then me!

CAROL. Help! Help! Phyllis!

HOWARD. If you don't shut that yap!

(HOWARD pulls back hammer.)

CAROL. Howard, don't! Don't!

HOWARD. Give me one good reason why we should both live?

CAROL. Because we're human beings, Howard--fallible and often stupid but not evil--not really--just pathetic--mistaken-- desperate—

HOWARD. We're alone in the cosmos!

CAROL. Howard--this is not the cosmos--this is Central Park West!

HOWARD. No! It's not use! I want to die!

(HOWARD pulls the trigger at his own head and at CAROL, but the gun jams and continues to jam as he keeps pulling the trigger.)

HOWARD. God damn it! It's old--it's too old--like we'll be soon! It's broken down! It doesn't work!

CAROL. *(Softly.)* Howard, give me the gun. Give it to me. *(CAROL pulls the gun away from HOWARD.)* You lunatic! What's the matter with you!? I'm shaking like a leaf! I'm trembling, I feel faint! I need a valium—

(PHYLLIS enters from SL. She is oblivious to what has been going on.)

PHYLLIS. What's all the noise--I thought I said out.

CAROL. *(Shaken.)* Howard just tried to kill both of us--first me and then himself--with his father's pistol--a souvenir--but--but--but--it jammed--he pulled the trigger--but--it jammed—

(PHYLLIS picks up the pistol and fools with it.)

PHYLLIS. There's nothing wrong with this gun, Howard.
You forgot to unlock the safety catch.
CAROL. Oh, God!

*(CAROL runs off USL. PHYLLIS sits with HOWARD on the
couch.)*

PHYLLIS. The truth is, Howard, that even though you are
suffering from one of your clinical depressions you are cor-
rect to be depressed. Even a clock that is broken is right twice
a day. Depressing things have happened to you. First you put
your dear, sweet father in a second rate home for the aged—
HOWARD. It's not second rate.
PHYLLIS. Face it, Howard, the best of them are none too
good, but the one you chose, sensibly within your budget, is--
and you'll understand this--a schlock house. Following the
experience of parting with a parent, which by the way, brings
you psychologically one step closer to realization of the end
of your own life--your wife is abandoning you for your good
friend--a successful male with a higher testosterone level--
whom of course she has been diddling for two years behind
your back. So it's almost healthy for you to be depressed. If
you were not depressed, you'd be an idiot. Am I being help-
ful?
HOWARD. I miss my son...
PHYLLIS. I give this whole thing six months.
HOWARD. Sam and Carol? They may move to London.
PHYLLIS. Six months whether it's London or Tierra Del
Fuego. They're both too defective.

HOWARD. I knew he fooled around.

PHYLLIS. Did you?

HOWARD. Who didn't?

PHYLLIS. Just me I suppose.

HOWARD. I think just you, Phyllis--I think I even heard a dirty innuendo from a bus boy at Twenty One.

PHYLLIS. The bus boy knew?

HOWARD. Naturally he didn't know I knew Sam or you and Sam was entering and I was having lunch and I saw the bus boy nudge the waiter and nod toward Sam and point to a sexy brunette and he said, "What a nerve--he's banging her and yet he comes in with his wife all the time." I was surprised he knew the term "banging" because he was just over from Poland.

PHYLLIS. That's a great story, Howard. The waiter and the Polish bus boy knew but not me.

(The door opens and SAM enters.)

SAM. *(Coldly firm.)* I came to get the rest of my papers--*(Seeing them.)* Oh Jesus, what did you do?

PHYLLIS. I need a few answers from you, big shot.

SAM. You had your go at me. I tried the reasonable route. I'm not getting my skull fractured by an hysteric—

HOWARD. You've been carrying on with my wife for two years.

SAM. You I'll talk to, Howard, and I'll start with an apology.

PHYLLIS. Oh, that just makes it all ok, doesn't it?

SAM. I said I didn't want to hear from you. I'm here to get my papers--look what you've done...

HOWARD. I can't easily accept your apology, Sam, because we're supposed to be close.

SAM. *(Angry at PHYLLIS.)* I have some complicated cases going—

PHYLLIS. So you were screwing all my friends.

SAM. These last couple of years have not been easy for me, Phyllis--my work has not gone well. Why did you tear up everything?

PHYLLIS. I said, so you were screwing all my friends—

SAM. No, I wasn't screwing all your friends—

PHYLLIS. Liar! I know--I know everything!

SAM. Well, if you know everything you don't need me to tell you anything. Now will you get your foot off my paper-- get it off--*(Forces it off.)* Get it off!

PHYLLIS. Ouch--you bastard!

SAM. I gave you a chance to talk things out--I poured my guts out to you today--and where'd it get me?

PHYLLIS. I trusted you. How am I supposed to know that underneath you're seething with discontent. If only you had been honest instead of letting your gripes fester and taking up with my friends.

HOWARD. *(Rising pugnaciously.)* I'm angry at you, Sam- -you made me a cuckold—

SAM. *(Pushes him down.)* Sit down, Howard. We can talk later. I said I apologize.

PHYLLIS. I know you slept with Edith and Helene--what about Polly?

SAM. You're cuckoo. I am so glad to be out of this.

PHYLLIS. You're not out yet, Sugar.

SAM. As soon as I get this mess together, I'm history.

HOWARD. She knows about the brunette at Twenty-One--

with the bangs and the full lips.

SAM. Howard, I'm sorry about me and Carol--I honestly didn't think you'd ever find out.

PHYLLIS. *(Turning on SAM.)* What about my sister?

SAM. What?

PHYLLIS. What about Susan?

SAM. What about Susan?

PHYLLIS. Did you sleep with her too?

SAM. You're hallucinating.

PHYLLIS. Hallucinating. *(To HOWARD.)* That's the word he used to deny Carol when I found the Filofax.

SAM. Because it was absurd.

PHYLLIS. How absurd can it be? If you were sleeping with Carol, why not Susan? Now it all comes back to me. I used to notice you stare at her--and she always went to watch you play softball in East Hampton.

HOWARD. What kind of woman are you, Phyllis, that all these seemingly close people willingly betray you.

PHYLLIS. *(Stopped by this, regains poise.)* You need shock treatment, Howard. Why don't you wet your finger and stick it in the socket.

SAM. I'm gathering my papers and I'm out of here. I am out--out--for good--and forever.

PHYLLIS. *(Goes to phone.)* I'm calling Susan—

SAM. Put that down!

(SAM takes the phone from PHYLLIS, hangs up.)

PHYLLIS. Look at the nostrils flare. He's scared.

SAM. Scared of what? I'm finished in your life.

PHYLLIS. *(Taking phone again.)* Hey, lover, a girl can call her sister, can't she?

SAM. If you insist on making a fool of yourself...

PHYLLIS. *(Dials.)* My first husband appreciated women too but he didn't act out--may he rest in peace--or Tel Aviv or wherever the hell he's living--*(On phone.)* Hello, Donald, put Susan on—

SAM. I can't believe she can still rattle me—

(SAM pours himself a drink.)

HOWARD. She's a ball buster--but you did some evil things, Sam.

SAM. I did zero.

PHYLLIS. *(On phone.)* Susan--did you have an affair with Sam? I'm asking you if you had an affair with Sam?... When you stayed here... Well, I don't buy it, Susan!... I say you did-- I say that was your way of getting even with me...

HOWARD. Even for what? Did you sleep with Susan's husband?

PHYLLIS. *(To HOWARD.)* Of course I didn't sleep with Susan's husband. *(Into phone.)* What?--No, I didn't sleep with Donald! Would I sleep with and Orthodox Freudian? But you did with Sam! Because you're a gypsy--a lost soul--and it was my generosity that kept you afloat and you resented me and this is the way you repay me!

(PHYLLIS hangs up angrily.)

SAM. Bravo--and now that you've made yourself an ass in her eyes because, baby doll—

PHYLLIS. Don't call me baby doll—

SAM. Because, Godzilla, I never laid a finger on Susan.
HOWARD. Who *was* that brunette at Twenty One?
SAM. Howard, why don't you get some rest?

(Enter CAROL, surprised to SAM.)

CAROL. Sam.
SAM. Hello, Carol.
CAROL. Phyllis and Howard know everything. It has been quite a night.
HOWARD. It's like a boil was lanced and all the pus is coming out.
CAROL. Can we go, Sam? I need an hour to pack at home.
SAM. Go where?
CAROL. To our apartment, to Amagansett, if you want, straight to London--I just don't care anymore.
SAM. I don't understand--where are we going?
CAROL. Out of here--look, we all clearly need new lives--not just Sam and me--but Phyllis and Howard--I say we look at tonight as a beginning--we don't have to give in to our bleakest thoughts. I know--it sounds easy for me to say because Sam and I have each other--but I say we can be civilized and help one another get through this.
SAM. Just a minute--we're not going away—
CAROL. Well, you mentioned London--I mean away is just out of here.
SAM. Carol, I think you misunderstood.
CAROL. What?
SAM. I met someone and I'm in love.
CAROL. What do you mean?
SAM. I met a woman and I'm in love.

CAROL. I don't understand--you're in love with me.

SAM. No--we had a fling but--we never were in love.

CAROL. I am.

SAM. Oh but--I never--you thought I was leaving Phyllis for you?

CAROL. Sam—

PHYLLIS. Sometimes there's God so quickly.

SAM. Carol--I was crystal clear on that point--at least I thought I was.

CAROL. *(Staggering.)* Legs--legs--the room is spinning-- I feel faint—

HOWARD. Get some smelling salts. Ha, ha, ha...

(HOWARD is laughing.)

PHYLLIS. *(To CAROL.)* Honey, what *were* you thinking?

CAROL. Sam--Sam--all those afternoons--we talked—

SAM. But that was the whole point--we were both just having a fling.

CAROL. That's how it started—

SAM. And it never changed.

CAROL. Of course it did.

SAM. Of course it didn't.

HOWARD. This is truly comical.

(HOWARD is amused by it all.)

CAROL. But all the talk about the future--and London—

SAM. But that was just speculating--there was no actual plan—

CAROL. There was—

SAM. There couldn't have been--we never had that kind of a relationship.

CAROL. Of course we did—

SAM. We were never in love--at least I wasn't.

CAROL. You told me you were—

SAM. Carol-- you're dreaming—

CAROL. "I've got to end my marriage--I'm suffocating--I'm drowning--the time with you is the only thing that keeps me alive—"

SAM. In the context of illicit sex--I told you the ground rules from day one.

CAROL. Yes--but--it--it--seemed to change--to deepen--you asked me if I could be happy in London?

SAM. Carol, you're reading into it—

CAROL. *(Total realization.)* You bastard--you used me.

PHYLLIS. *(Annoyed.)* How was I suffocating you? Why were you drowning? Huh? You clown.

HOWARD. *(Getting jollier.)* He's a clown--this is a circus, he's a clown--and we're all freaks.

CAROL. You lied to me--you lied to me—

PHYLLIS. You got what you deserved, you crypto-hooker.

CAROL. "I want to be with you, Carol--with you I'm happy--with you I know my only real moments--rescue me from that self-centered storm trooper who's crushed my hopes—"

PHYLLIS. A Nazi? Did you tell her I was a Nazi?

SAM. *(Innocently.)* I never said you were a party member.

CAROL. I don't believe this! I don't believe you can make love like that without feeling love.

PHYLLIS. A stiff prick knows no conscience.

CAROL. *(Shattered.)* This was real--this was true...

SAM. *(Turning on CAROL.)* Carol, don't hold me responsible for your wishful thinking! I was above board down the line.

CAROL. No—

PHYLLIS. A woman with a tenuous grasp of reality...

CAROL. You're the one with no grasp of reality. Deluded into thinking you had your marriage under control while he's off with everybody.

SAM. That's enough, Carol.

CAROL. In your own bed with Nancy Rice.

PHYLLIS. Nancy Rice is on the ethics committee!

SAM. *(To CAROL.)* What good does it do to provoke?

PHYLLIS. Nancy Rice is chairwoman of the ethics committee at the hospital--her specialty is moral choice.

SAM. Yes, I had a quick moment with Nancy Rice when you were in Denver but she instigated it. And you and I had no more sex life to speak of.

PHYLLIS. Now I know why--a man cannot ejaculate every day in triple figures.

SAM. That's not the reason!

PHYLLIS. No? What's the reason?

SAM. What's the reason? What are we yelling for?

PHYLLIS What's the reason our lovemaking disappeared like vapor?

SAM. You want to know the reason?

PHYLLIS. Yes--yes--the reason. Tell me the goddamned reason.

SAM. The spontaneity went out of it.

PHYLLIS. You think you're talking to a retard? I'm not her. *(Meaning CAROL.)*

HOWARD. Hey--one thing Carol is not is retarded—

CAROL. Oh Howard—

HOWARD. She has a learning disability but that's different.

CAROL. Will you shut up, Howard!

HOWARD. Hey--back off--I was explaining why you might *seem* retarded but aren't.

CAROL. Shut up! Will you shut your mouth? Just shut up!! *(To PHYLLIS.)* He turned off you because you don't care enough to please a man sexually. Am I lying, Sam? Or did you not use the term nude catatonic?

SAM. Mind your business.

HOWARD. I think the problem is Phyllis can be castrating.

SAM. Will you get back in the woodwork.

HOWARD. You told me as much, Sam. When you get drunk over lunch you babble--Where did the time go? What happened to all my promise? Should I feel like Mr. Phyllis Riggs?

PHYLLIS. What is this madness? I'm penalized by everyone because I'm a success? My sister, my friends, my husband—

HOWARD. People never hate you for your weaknesses--they hate you for your strengths.

CAROL. Sam, you led me on--you said you loved me.

SAM. Never—

CAROL. Yes—

SAM. Never—

CAROL. Yes—

SAM. I was careful. I never used that word.

PHYLLIS. Never fuck a lawyer, they get you on the terminology.

HOWARD. I can beat Sam in racquetball.

SAM. Sure you can, Howard.

HOWARD. *(Putting on music.)* It drives him crazy--he's muscular but not coordinated.

SAM. Uh-huh.

CAROL. Sam, I had everything planned--you were going to leave Phyllis.

HOWARD. He did, Carol, aren't you paying attention.

CAROL. Shut up, you manic psychotic!

HOWARD. Everyone's so down—

(HOWARD turns up the music.)

CAROL. Turn that off! Turn it off! Off! Stop! Sam, turn it off!!!

(SAM turns off the music.)

HOWARD. What's gotten into everybody--you'd think there was a funeral.

SAM. Howard, calm down.

HOWARD. Everyone's so cranky--probably 'cause you're hungry--Why don't I whip up something?

CAROL. Idiot!

HOWARD. What?

CAROL. Idiot! Fool!

HOWARD. I'm sorry I can't help it, I'm famished.

(HOWARD exits SR into kitchen.)

CAROL. I cared for you, Sam--I loved you--do love you—

SAM. I didn't mean to lead you on--I tried to be careful--I'm not out to hurt anybody.

(The door bell rings--CAROL, nearest to the door, opens it, admitting a very young, beautiful, lovely, sexy woman named JULIET POWELL.)

JULIET. *(To SAM.)* I was waiting downstairs and I got worried--I know you almost had your head bashed in before and I--when you didn't come down—

PHYLLIS. No--no--no.

CAROL. Is this her?

JULIET. I debated coming up but you said five minutes—

SAM. This is her--she--Juliet Powell--Carol--Phyllis--well, Dr. Riggs needs no introduction—

PHYLLIS. No introduction. Just drive me to Bellevue and check me in.

CAROL. Do you know each other?

SAM. Look--let's just lay this all on the line and try to wrap it up with no bullshit. Juliet is--was--a patient of Phyllis's, okay?

PHYLLIS. When did you—

SAM. *(To CAROL.)* Once a long time ago I happened to notice her in the waiting room--I have my own private access but every once in a blue moon I glimpse one of Phyllis's wounded either coming or going, in tears or just sitting there reading *Town and Country*. And I remember thinking, my God-- what a lovely creature--so young and fresh--what problems can she possibly have at her age? And then, as fate would have it, several weeks ago I left the apartment at the same time Juliet emerged from the elevator to enter for her session--and I spoke to her--just hello--but knowing she'd be coming down in fifty minutes--I bought a paper and sat on the park bench across the street and sure enough--fifty-two minutes later on the dot she emerged and I said hello again--what a surprise--and now I'm going to marry her.

PHYLLIS. *(To JULIET.)* And I'm going to stop being a shrink and become a chiropractor.

JULIET. *(Ingenuously.)* That's why I quit treatment. I didn't think it was realistic to continue my analysis with you while I was...

PHYLLIS. Fucking my husband? Good, thank you Miss Teenage America.

CAROL. Sam, she could be your daughter.

SAM. Yes--but she's not. She's the daughter of Mr. and Mrs. Morton Powell who I don't know from a hole in the wall. Unless you read *The Wall Street Journal.*

CAROL. But what can you possibly have in common?

SAM. You'd be surprised. This is a charming, educated, twenty-five year old—

JULIET. Twenty-one—

SAM. Well, soon to be twenty-five--four years goes like that—

CAROL. What is it that you do, Miss Powell?

JULIET. Do?

CAROL. Your--line of work...

JULIET. Oh--film editor. I mean I will be when I graduate.

CAROL. Which high school?

JULIET. No--Barnard College. I should have been out but I took a year's hiatus.

PHYLLIS. Miss Powell has had some severe emotional problems.

JULIET. Yes, well—

PHYLLIS. She came to me a year ago--introverted, confused, anorexic--petrified of men. My goal was to liberate her so she could emerge as a woman and function.

JULIET. Yes and you did it.

PHYLLIS. Yes, I noticed.

JULIET. It's terrible because I hate to lose you as an analyst. Oh--but on the other hand, you always tried to guide me to act in my own best interests.

PHYLLIS. And you think my middle-aged husband is in your best interests?

JULIET. Well, at first I did have some uncomfortable dreams--the spider dream again--only this time, *you* were the black widow, my mother was the scorpion, and--Carol was the tarantula.

CAROL. But you didn't even know me.

JULIET. Well, Sam told me about you and of course that gave rise to all of these fantasies.

CAROL. A tarantula—

JULIET. Hairy and grasping--Oh, I mean he didn't describe you that way--it was just conclusions that my unconscious drew from whatever he did say—

CAROL. Hairy and grasping—

JULIET. But in answer to your question--yes--I had reservations--but Sam described a long dead marriage and I didn't seem to be coming between anybody--I mean he was already sleeping with Carol and Mrs. Bucksbaum.

PHYLLIS. Who?

JULIET. Mrs. Bucksbaum? The lady on two?

PHYLLIS. Oh, Sam--she's crippled!

SAM. What does that mean? For Chrissake, Phyllis--I understand it was not noble of me to cheat but not because the woman has a short leg.

PHYLLIS. How'd you do it with her? Did you stand her on a box?

CAROL. *(To SAM.)* Why am I hairy and grasping? How have I grasped? I gave myself--I gave and I gave--I ran when you called--I broke appointments--I told lies--I juggled my schedule to accommodate and demanded nothing--how could you give her the impression that I was a tarantula?

SAM. How am I responsible for what she dreams about you?

CAROL. Do you realize the kind of man you're going to marry?

JULIET. Well, actually marriage is more Sam's idea--I'm just content to see how things go.

SAM. No--I want the commitment--I need it--I can't go on like this--I want something stable for once--I have to bring some sanity to my life. Juliet, you're everything that I have ever dreamed of.

CAROL. A twenty year old?! In publishing?

SAM. Editing--she's a film editor.

PHYLLIS. Six months ago she couldn't look a man in the eye without getting shingles.

SAM. Look, I know what you're all thinking but this is the real thing. Despite what you two might say--I'm finished as a Don Juan. Promiscuity is no answer. Do you think a person is fulfilled by empty, cheap, stupid adultery?

CAROL. Thanks, Sam, it was meaningful for me too.

SAM. *(To JULIET.)* All I'm trying to say is I found you Juliet and I want this to be forever.

PHYLLIS. What about when she's my age? You'll be gumming your food on Medicare.

CAROL. I know I'm not young and beautiful but this is too much to take--this is more than I can handle!

HOWARD. *(Popping in.)* I decided to make ravioli--it's the only thing you have—

CAROL. My life is a shambles—

HOWARD. Too bad there's no pesto--but I can do a cream sauce and I'll do small tossed salads with anchovies and balsamic vinegar--who's this?

JULIET. *(Shaking hands with HOWARD.)* I'm Juliet Powell.

HOWARD. Hi, I'm Howard.

JULIET. See, six months ago I couldn't have just introduced myself.

SAM. Tell me that you're not wavering on our marriage. I need the reassurance.

JULIET. I just want us to be sure, that's all. Why isn't it enough if we keep seeing each other and see where it takes us?

SAM. You're reneging. I thought we'd settled it. Last night you felt certain.

HOWARD. *(To JULIET.)* What do you want to get married for? You're a kid.

SAM. Howard—

HOWARD. No, I'm serious--she's a kid and you're ancient--ancient, I don't mean ancient but you're much too old for her.

SAM. That's our business.

HOWARD. And you come to her with such baggage--all those scars and bitterness--fixed in your ways.

SAM. I'm not bitter, Howard, I just want to start over.

HOWARD. Hey, who wouldn't? *(To JULIET.)* Marriage is a huge step for anyone--much less a kid like you and a screwed up middle-aged Cassanova.

JULIET. I keep telling him I think we should wait.

SAM. I want you.

HOWARD. He's nervous because he knows you'll meet somebody else.

SAM. Will you butt out--*(To JULIET.)* The man is certifiable.

HOWARD. Not so fast. I hear what this young woman is saying--you're pushing too hard. *(To JULIET.)* What do you need marriage for anyhow? You don't want to lock yourself in with any one guy--you should be out tasting life--you're only a kid once.

JULIET. The truth is I'm just coming out of my shell, thanks to Phyllis.

PHYLLIS. If it's thanks to me, *I'm* joining the Hemlock Society. And stop calling me Phyllis--I'm still Dr. Riggs.

CAROL. *(Running to SAM, hitting him.)* I'm a spider? I'm a hairy, grasping spider?!

SAM. Carol, get off my back.

HOWARD. All I'm saying is she should not be thinking of marriage and especially to you. Remember, Juliet--marriage is the death of hope.

JULIET. The death of hope--what a poetic way to put it.

HOWARD. Actually I'm a writer.

SAM. *(To HOWARD.)* It was the death of hope for you, Howard--for us it's a bright future.

JULIET. *He* brought up marriage--I just got confused.

HOWARD. Juliet, may I call you Juliet?--If this guy's talking life time commitment, take my advice and run for your life--your young life--after all, you're so pretty and so appetizing--so luscious and succulent—

PHYLLIS. For Chrissake, Howard, you sound like you want to cook her.

SAM. I can't believe you're giving him a shred of credibility. He's a cartoon.

JULIET. I told you, Sam, I've never had an affair before—

HOWARD. Many men will fall in love with you--you're very lovely--I could and we just met.

SAM. He's competing with me--I can't believe it--he's competing.

HOWARD. What do you plan to do with your life?

JULIET. I'd like to be a film editor.

HOWARD. Hey--perfect for me! You know, I've written a number of screenplays.

SAM. None that ever sold--oh yes--and a novel.

JULIET. *(Impressed.)* You wrote a novel? How wonderful.

SAM. *(Losing it a little.)* Instantly remaindered. A thinly disguised novel about an ex-college athlete who's competitive with a brilliant foul-mouthed wife who heads the department of a hospital and writes books and is the center of attention wherever they go and who never realizes he's weak and she is inadvertently emasculating the poor bastard so all he lives for is illicit sex.

PHYLLIS. With the physically and mentally handicapped.

HOWARD. Juliet, I have a number of wonderful possibilities on the coast--Actually I expect a call tomorrow from Paramount—

SAM. He's delusional, Juliet--he's got nothing--he *is* nothing.

JULIET. I think I feel a migraine coming on—

SAM. This is incredible. What started out as a minor annoyance has snowballed into a catastrophe. Juliet, I love you. We vowed it would be forever--now let's go.

HOWARD. Not so fast, Sam. Juliet and I have real potential.

SAM. He's nuts--he's an emotional yo-yo. In ten minutes you'll be pulling him in off the window ledge.

HOWARD. Think about California with me. All I have to do is say yes to a very big deal at MGM.

JULIET. Didn't you say Paramount?

HOWARD. *(Talking very fast.)* I have a great notion for a film although once you have a hit they press you for a three picture deal. I have some high concept ideas--one I'd like to direct. There's always been quite a bit of interest in me as a director but I've always said no. Still, I might consider it-- provided they sweeten the pot. You can do the editing. I'll wire my real estate broker in Beverly Hills and we'll rent a house, it's silly to buy at first--you never know how long you're staying--Of course we'll get something spacious--maybe in Bel Air--I'd love an Olympic sized swimming pool--it'll be fun for the kids--Actually I think I read that Warren Beatty might be selling his home. Warren's a very dear friend of mine. Not that we've spent a lot of time together but we met at a political rally--*(Looks at watch.)* Why don't I call him--let's see, it's three hours earlier there—

SAM. *(Has had enough, he grabs JULIET.)* Juliet, let's get out of here!

HOWARD. *(Stops him.)* Hey--not so fast.

SAM. Get out of the way, Howard.

HOWARD. No, Sam--you can't always have your way.

SAM. I said we're leaving.

JULIET. Now just a minute here--I'm feeling anxious—

SAM. Alright--I'm leaving--we can discuss it in the car.

HOWARD. Leave her alone.

SAM. Howard...

HOWARD. I mean it, Sam, I will not let this girl be pushed around. I mean to spend the rest of my life with her.

SAM. I said out of my way!

(SAM pushes HOWARD and a scuffle ensues which gets more and more serious to the surprise of everyone.)

PHYLLIS. All right--knock it off--we're not in the jungle--This is Central Park West.
JULIET. Stop it--leave him alone!
HOWARD. You're strangling me—
PHYLLIS. Stop it—
JULIET. Please--I cant' stand it! Stop!--Stop!--Stop!

(There is a general ad-lib trying to object and stop it. JULIET picks up the gun and shoots SAM. Screams.)

SAM. Oh my God!
PHYLLIS. Sam!
JULIET. What happened!? It went off!
SAM. I have a terrific pain in my backside.
PHYLLIS. Get an ambulance—
JULIET. I didn't mean to—
PHYLLIS. (To CAROL.) Call an ambulance!
JULIET. Everything went red—
CAROL. This morning I thought you loved me. Now I can't tell you how much pleasure it gives me that you got shot in the ass.
PHYLLIS. Get out of here now--before the police come--just walk out the door calmly and go home.
JULIET. I'm awfully sorry, Sam.
SAM. What is a German Lugar doing on my living room table?!
HOWARD. Why don't I whip up some Babaganoush?

PHYLLIS. (To JULIET.) Go--the police will come--they'll see that you're the pretty daughter of a known Wall Street banker and they'll lick their lips and phone the press—

JULIET. I didn't mean it--it was an accident.

PHYLLIS. There are no accidents, baby. You still need me to tell you that? Now go home and stay home. We'll discuss this Monday. (To CAROL.) Give me that!

CAROL. Howard, get your coat. We're going home. The Movie Channel is showing "The Island Of Lost Souls." I want to see if our names come up.

HOWARD. Can we stop at Zabar's?

CAROL. Sure. Why not.

JULIET. Good-bye, Dr. Riggs. See you Monday at our usual time—

SAM. Juliet--Juliet--don't go--I love you—

(As lights fade.)

PHYLLIS. Grow up, Sam--she shot you in the ass--it's called rejection!

Fade to Black

END OF PLAY

<u>COSTUME PLOT</u>

SAM
Gray flannel suit q/blood red handkerchief in pocket
Silver sports watch
Maroon striped shirt
Black lace up shoes

HOWARD
Tweedy jacket'
Greeny pants
Duffel coat
Cream checked Tatersall shirt
Knit tie
Olive green cap
Brown leather gloves
Brown socks
Dark brown belt
Brown banded watch
Dark brown suede shoes
V-neck t shirts (under all)
Adds apron during play; removes clothing throughout play
Brown tortoiseshell glasses

CAROL
Navy blue Calvin Klein dress
Navy hat
Floral scarf
Earrings
Necklace

Fauz Rolex watch
Gold coat w/scarf
Navy blue leather gloves
Small blue Coach bag
Navy opaque hose
Black slinky underwear/leotards
Possibly Warner's nude leotard
Wedding band
Emerald ring
Giorgio Armani blue cloth shoes
Other jewelry as added

PHYLLIS
Green pantsuit
Maroon suede shoes
Maroon socks
Large tortoiseshell glasses
Purple wristwatch
1 necklace
3 bracelets: 1 ivory, 1 beaten silver, 1 jade
Silver earrings
Several silver rings (use as wedding band)

JULIET
Dress
Carry gray jacket
Black loafers
Black hose
Earrings

PROPERTY PLOT

Sofa
Ottoman
Arm chair
Side table

Coffee table
    Brief case w/Files, Filofax
            8 Blue Documents, 6 File folders, 1 NY Times section
    Check book

Parsons Table
    Phone
    2 decorative boxes

Bar Cart
    Glasses
    Water Pitcher w/water
    Vodka Bottle w/ water
    Chivas Bottle w/tea
            Preset: Water, Mug, Kleenex for Kelly Off Left

Writing Desk w/address book, wooden box, stamp dispenser SL
Trash Can
Art Work on pedestal UL

2 Chairs SR--US chair knocked over
Round Table w/bowl of almonds and lamp SR
            CHECK: Water spills + Tic Tacs DR

Stereo Console SR
Dried flowers in Fireplace UC
1 Framed painting on SR Wall
2 Framed paintings on SL Wall
1 Painted Wall hanging UC over fireplace

1 Amenhotep statue on floor w/receipts SL
Assorted receipts on floor SL

1 Bergdorf Bag preset UL
1 Glass off Left w/sip of water
1 Luger gun off Right
1 Starter pistols off Right (loaded) w/ear plugs

TOP OF *CPW*: Kill Running Lights

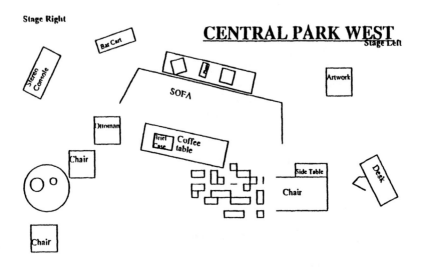

Stage Right

CENTRAL PARK WEST

Stage Left

Stereo Console

Bar Cart

SOFA

Artwork

Ottoman

Chair

Brief Case

Coffee table

Side Table

Chair

Desk

Chair

Brief case· 8 Blue-backed legal documents (face down)
6 Manilla folders with 2 sheets of paper inside each.
1 Filo fax
1 Business section of NY TIMES.

Sofa
Ottoman
Arm chair
Side Table
Coffee Table w/Brief case/ckbook
Parsons Table w/Phone and
    2 Decorative Boxes
Bar Cart w/glasses, Water Pitcher,
    2 Absolut, 1 Chivas
Writing Desk SL w/address book,
    wooden box, stamp disp.
Trash can
Art work on pedestal UL
2 chairs SR (1 knocked over)
1 round table w/lamp & nuts
Stereo Console SR
Dried flowers in Fireplace UC
1 Framed painting on SR wall
2 Framed paintings on SL wall
1 Painted Wall Hanging UC
1 Amenhotep statue on floor SL
Assorted Receipts on floor SL

1 Bergdorf Bag preset UL
1 Glass Off Left w/sip water
1 Luger Gun Off Right
2 Starter Pistols Off Right

Bar Cart Top Level

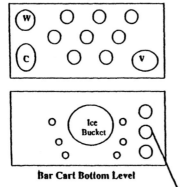

W

C

V

Ice Bucket

Bar Cart Bottom Level

Extra Bottle Absolut

Works by
David Mamet...

American Buffalo
Bobby Gould In Hell
The Cherry Orchard (Adapted by)
Dark Pony
Death Defying Acts
The Disappearance of the Jews
Dramatic Sketches and Monologues
The Duck Variations
Edmond
The Frog Prince
Glengarry Glen Ross
Goldberg Street
Keep Your Pantheon
Lakeboat
A Life in the Theatre
The Luftmensch
Mr. Happiness
November
The Old Neighborhood
One Way Street
The Poet and the Rent
Race
Reunion
The Sanctity of Marriage
School
Sexual Perversity in Chicago
The Shawl
Speed-the-Plow
Squirrels
The Three Sisters (Adapted by)
Uncle Vanya (Adapted by)
The Water Engine
The Woods

Please visit our website **samuelfrench.com** for complete descriptions and licensing information.

OTHER TITLES AVAILABLE FROM SAMUEL FRENCH

BOBBY GOULD IN HELL

David Mamet

Short Play, Comedy / 3m, 1f / Interior

This is Bobby Gould's day of reckoning. The conniving movie mogul from *Speed the Plow* awakes in a strange room. A loquacious interrogator in fishing waders enters. Gould argues his case. A woman he has wronged appears and gets so carried away that she says some sassy things to the Interrogator. In the end, Bobby is damned for being "cruel without being interesting."

"Funny and pungent."
– *The New York Times*

"Lifts the soul."
– *New York Daily News*

"Hilarious... with flashy magic tricks."
– *Newsday*

Published with *The Devil and Billy Markham*
by Shel Silverstein in *Oh, Hell!*

OTHER TITLES AVAILABLE FROM SAMUEL FRENCH

THE POET AND THE RENT

David Mamet

Drama / 8m, 3f, extras (doubling possible) / Simple set

David, a young poet behind in his rent and about to be evicted, improvises poems for money in the park. He is scorned by the public and he falls in love with a young woman who will have nothing to do with him. He becomes a nightwatchman and is robbed by thieves who talk him into joining them. Apprehended by the police and jailed, he is visited by a man who heard his poems – an ad executive who offers David a job writing ad copy for Wacko, noxious gook for cars. Faced with his first existential choice, he decides to languish in jail rather than promote Wacko. The young woman pays his bail and rent. She still finds him socially undesirable, but feels all good citizens should support the arts. A better man, David returns to his pen and paper.

OTHER TITLES AVAILABLE FROM SAMUEL FRENCH

SPEED-THE-PLOW

David Mamet

Dramatic Comedy / 2m, 1f / 2 interiors, simply suggested

Revived on Broadway in 2008, the original production starred Joe Mantegna, Ron Silver and Madonna in this hilarious satire of Hollywood, a culture as corrupt as the society it claims to reflect. Charlie Fox has a terrific vehicle for a currently hot client. Bringing the script to his friend Bobby Gould, the newly appointed Head of Production at a major studio, both see the work as their ticket to the Big Time. The star wants to do it; as they prepare their pitch to the studio boss, Bobby wagers Charlie that he can seduce the temp/secretary, Karen. As a ruse, he gives her a novel by "some Eastern sissy" writer that needs a courtesy read before being dismissed out of hand. Karen slyly determines the novel, not the movie-star script, should be the company's next film. She sleeps with Bobby who is so smitten with Karen and her ideals that he pleads with Charlie to drop the star project and and pitch the "Eastern sissy" writer's book.

"Hilarious and chilling ."
– *The New York Times*

"Mamet's clearest, wittiest play."
– *The New York Daily News*

"I laughed and laughed. The play is crammed with wonderful, dazzling, brilliant lines."
– *The New York Post*

OTHER TITLES AVAILABLE FROM SAMUEL FRENCH

THE WATER ENGINE

David Mamet

An American Fable / 6m, 2f / Interior

As the audience watches, actors, an announcer and a sound effects man present a radio play during the 1930s with unerring authenticity. The "play within the play" reveals the story of a young inventor who's found a way to run an engine on distilled water. At first ridiculed, he is courted by crooked lawyers attempting to buy the invention from him on behalf of 'certain business interests'. Refusing, he is threatened and when he attempts to give his story to the newspapers, is murdered along with his sister. The engine is destroyed, but the inventor has mailed the blueprint to a young student scientist who will configure and reveal his invention to the world.

"Extraordinary...verbal brilliance."
– *The New York Times*

"A vivid theatrical experience."
– *New York Daily News*

Published with *Mr. Happiness*

CPSIA information can be obtained at www.ICGtesting.com
Printed in the USA
BVOW02s0816080813

328161BV00012B/114/P

9 780573 695391